DATE DUE

~~AP 5 '96~~		
~~OE 1 00~~		

DEMCO 38-296

C. Margaret Hall, PhD, CCS

New Families: Reviving and Creating Meaningful Bonds

*Pre-publication
REVIEWS,
COMMENTARIES,
EVALUATIONS . . .*

"**D**efining family as a primary source of self, gender, and ethnicity, the author illustrates how "new families" redefine traditional values and how new can be distinguished from nuclear and traditional families. Through exhaustive clinical and academic research, Doctor Hall has identified a type of family that is associated with progress, growth, change, and survival based on *flexibility*.

Although individuals are paradoxically emotionally dependent on those family members assigned to foster their growth and independence, Hall describes in great detail the challenge to individual fulfillment of New Families: to become healthily interdependent rather than unhealthily overdependent in family relations. In a contemporary society of increasing complexity *New Families* crystallizes what's happening in one's own family."

Edward W. Beal, MD
*Clinical Associate Professor,
Georgetown University School
of Medicine*

More pre-publication
REVIEWS, COMMENTARIES, EVALUATIONS . . .

"In *New Families*, C. Margaret Hall brings a wealth of clinical experience to describing the changing profile of families in modern America. Hall argues that "traditional" and "nuclear" families are plagued by rigidities and narrow definitions of acceptable behavior. By contrast, "new families" display more flexible gender roles, minimal authority structures, and more fluid and open relationships. HALL'S ARGUMENT FLOWS BEAUTIFULLY AND LOGICALLY THROUGH THE PAGES OF THIS REMARKABLE BOOK: The family is the primary crucible of our identity; it takes many forms and shapes, but each one is uniquely worth exploring; our ability to move forward as independent, autonomous individuals depends on our willingness to grapple with the entire family portrait, not just the parts we like; and our emergent sense of who we are is inextricably rooted in our families, past and present.

But Hall's message is clear. If we avoid the conflicts, secrets, and hurts of family life, we also deny ourselves the opportunity to achieve the joy of true interconnectedness. This is a hard truth, and one that every reader will want to view from many angles and many readings of *New Families*.

Hall urges us to use time-honored techniques such as generating family trees and family histories, getting in touch with distant relatives, and even confronting the language of our own will-making as ways of expanding the boundaries of our families. Most of all, Hall's work helps us to see ourselves as part of an intricate web of relationships that forms the backdrop for our empowerment as individuals. This is a fascinating journey that ends with optimism toward the families of the next century."

Janet Mancini Billson, PhD, CCS
Assistant Executive Officer,
American Sociological Association;
Adjunct Professor of Sociology,
The George Washington University

The Haworth Press, Inc.

New Families
Reviving and Creating
Meaningful Bonds

HAWORTH Sociology

Marvin Sussman, PhD
Senior Editor

New, Recent, and Forthcoming Titles:

New Families: Reviving and Creating Meaningful Bonds
by C. Margaret Hall

New Families
Reviving and Creating Meaningful Bonds

C. Margaret Hall, PhD, CCS

The Haworth Press
New York • London • Norwood (Australia)

The Haworth Press, Inc., 10 Alice Street, Binghamton, NY 13904-1580

Library of Congress Cataloging-in-Publication Data

Hall, C. Margaret (Constance Margaret)
    New families : reviving and creating meaningful bonds / C. Margaret Hall.
       p.   cm.
    Includes bibliographical references and index.
    ISBN 1-56024-422-4 (alk. paper).
    1. Family life education. 3. Family. I. Title.
HQ10.H217   1993
306.85–dc20   92-44917
                                                      CIP

CONTENTS

ABOUT THE AUTHOR

C. Margaret Hall, PhD, CCS, is Professor of Sociology and Director of Women's Studies at Georgetown University. She has written extensively in the new field of clinical sociology, focusing primarily on the influence of family, gender, and religion or general beliefs on behavior. Dr. Hall has her own practice in clinical sociology and has organized and facilitated women's discussion groups. She belongs to the American Sociological Association, and the Sociological Practice Association.

Acknowledgements

I thank both my American and English families for being there, and for tolerating my somewhat erratic communications and participation over the years. Without the richness and emotional density of my own family experiences, I could not have discerned the patterns of behavior I describe in *New Families: Reviving and Creating Meaningful Bonds*.

Also vital to my endeavor, as well as personally significant, are the hundreds of individuals and families who gave me important details about the inner workings of their lives during my clinical work and research. Without this privileged, intimate knowledge I would not have had a sufficiently full understanding of family dependencies to write *New Families: Reviving and Creating Meaningful Bonds*.

The comprehensive and painstaking library research of Lisa McDonald and Brian Inglis kept me apprised of recent findings in contemporary family research. The clarity of their abstracts and extensive notes enabled me to distill large amounts of current literature about the changing family. Suzanne Baker's reviews of research on women were also invaluable aids in deepening my understanding of gender relations within families and society.

Mentors past and present–Murray Bowen, Marvin B. Sussman, Joan Aldous, D. H. J. Morgan, and Rev. John L. Thomas, S.J.– played a crucial role in sustaining my enthusiasm, interest, and rigor in family research over the long haul. They are inspiring examples. I particularly appreciate their extended conversations, which gave me both practical ideas and additional data.

Colleagues at the Georgetown Family Center directly and indirectly supported my efforts to compile *New Families: Reviving and Creating Meaningful Bonds*. Carolyn Moynihan, Jack Bradt, Marian Merrifield, Roberta Holt, Michael Kerr, Edward Beal, Charles Paddack, Lilian Rosenbaum, Roberta Gilbert, and Janet

Kuhn have all helped to strengthen my grasp of the complexities of family systems theory. Above all, they appreciate and endorse my efforts to address serious theoretical issues while coping with the inevitable intricacies of family data.

Elliott P. Skinner, of Columbia University, was the first of my colleagues to suggest that I write a practical book based on my family research. I am indebted to him for this idea, and trust that this book will be read and used outside specialized professional and academic circles as well as within.

Last, but not least, I thank Carol Gangnath, who read my entire manuscript. Her patience and goodwill helped me sustain my efforts, as did her timely corrections and suggestions.

Preface

New Families: Reviving and Creating Meaningful Bonds reviews and consolidates 22 years of my clinical work and research with families. Being a solution-oriented person, I have consistently sought to understand how families work best, and under which conditions family members are most satisfied with their lives. My professional responsibilities as a family therapist gave me many privileges and listening opportunities. I learned a great deal from the diverse reports of a wide variety of families. Furthermore, my particular specialization–crisis intervention–required that I know families as they really are, not as I (or they) might prefer families to be.

The core of my research effort during the past 22 years has been the development of identity empowerment theory. This core derives from my strong interest in the patterns of well-being shown by those "new" families that thrive impressively well in our society. These optimally functioning families are able to support the development and growth of all or most of their members. These families also facilitate the empowerment of their members' identities. This book is essentially a statement of the possible and probable benefits that can flow from the power and influence wielded by our families, whether we realize it or not, to define our being and behavior.

The generalizations and propositions in *New Families: Reviving and Creating Meaningful Bonds* are derived from data about a cross-section of different social classes and ethnic groups. However, my primary goal when interpreting these data was to delineate what I considered to be the most significant common denominators of family experiences, and the most viable directions for all families, rather than describe and explain the many specific differences among diverse social classes and ethnic groups. Just as we can fairly confidently surmise that most people are interested in pursuing some degree of happiness at some time in their lives, this book is based on the assumption that most people would choose to live in families which support growth and development.

Chapter 1

Introduction

New Families: Reviving and Creating Meaningful Bonds is a handbook for creating stronger, more meaningful bonds within our families. We can increase our freedom through interacting with relatives in empowering ways, rather than in self-defeating, ritualistic exchanges.

"New families" are defined as those families that are able to perpetuate themselves and thrive in spite of the many deleterious stresses in our highly industrialized society. These emergent and resilient new families are distinct from both traditional and nuclear families, in that they adapt successfully to technological change. We must understand and learn from these new families if our own family ties are to promote life and creativity–not inhibition and destructiveness–through our efforts to survive and be fulfilled (Ackerman, 1958).

New families emerge at every stage of evolution or history, and in every decade or year. Generally it is only *after* we have lived through a sufficiently long period of time, however, that we are able to evaluate families for what they really were and are. For example, immediately after World War II, we were not aware that political and social processes were hardening and splintering our nuclear families, nor did we recognize the underlying strains and stresses. Throughout the 1950s these families appeared to meet personal needs as well as society's demands for mobile workers and higher standards of living.

Similarly, the families that thrive today are functional adaptations to contemporary social changes. Accumulated clinical data suggest that some of these families will endure more effectively than others. In order to formulate optimal conditions for individual and family survival and fulfillment, this book focuses on the more resilient adaptive families.

Whether we like it or not, we are all dependent on those who are emotionally closest to us, whether they are spouses, live-in lovers, parents, brothers, sisters, children, grandparents, deceased relatives, or in-laws. Our challenge–and the pre-condition of our fulfillment–is to have healthfully interdependent, rather than overly dependent, family relationships.

This handbook uses family histories and information about past and present family crises as starting points for understanding our families more fully. This knowledge is crucial because we can only move fully into the future when we know our past sufficiently well to be able to intentionally let it go. *New Families: Reviving and Creating Meaningful Bonds* helps us examine and evaluate our family origins and roots, and moves us into the present and future, by directing our participation and interaction in intimate relationships and by motivating us to act in accordance with our own values and ideals.

Those new families that survive well in modern technological society must be able to withstand the pressures of high-speed living. They are stronger than traditional families, which have difficulty keeping up with rapid social changes. They are more durable than nuclear families, which tend to isolate parent-child groups, leaving them insufficiently resilient to adapt to everyday stresses. Nuclear families easily fragment and disintegrate while trying to cope with the complex strains of rapid change.

In order to understand the significance and characteristics of our emergent new families, we must consider the role of families in society in general, and in the United States in particular. The family is our most universal social institution; it continues to be linked to other social and political systems. Families magnify and reflect social patterns as well as provide vital sources of society's new life and new values (Aries, 1962). We create customs at the same time we battle everyday family problems (Berger & Kellner, 1977).

Obviously it is wise to try to ensure that our families work for us rather than against us. In many respects, families *will* give us some kind of support if we let them. We gain emotional security through realizing the interconnectedness of our past and present family relationships. We automatically benefit from strengthening family contacts that go beyond the two or three most familiar nuclear units (Sussman & Burchinal, 1962).

When we are more firmly connected to the networks of our past generations, we feel a stronger sense of identity with our ancestors. It is from the base of these interconnections that we create our own new families most effectively, new families that include all the relatives who are participants in our heritage. Our new families are ultimately our ethnic groups–the primary sources of our identities.

Families are particularly important because it is they who give us our first, and most persistent, definitions of self and gender. As children, we tend to either conform to–or rebel against–who our parents or significant others think we are. As adults, our challenge is to forge our own mature identities, and to journey toward the future through and beyond our family connections.

GENDER FLEXIBILITY

Permissiveness resulting from the sexual revolution of the 1970s, together with value changes due to feminist and human rights movements, has created an emotional climate where gender equality is more established as a norm and social ideal. New families derive from and reflect these shifts toward egalitarianism, thereby creating even greater gender flexibility.

When two spouses or two parents work together as a team, and value each other's companionship, their families will inevitably have open relationship systems which foster responsibility and autonomy among their members. It is essentially the lived reality of egalitarianism between spouses that predisposes entire families to treat girls and boys, or women and men, more equally. In the long run, these internal family dynamics have an impact on gender relations in the wider society; egalitarianism becomes more pervasive in attitudes, behavior, and social institutions.

Two different families are described below in order to illustrate the complex nuances of gender relations and gender flexibility within new families. Although older family members may play a crucial role in establishing the tone and direction of gender exchanges at different generational levels, the examples given are based only on younger family members.

Marvin and Nancy had already lived together for five years when they married in their early thirties. They were accustomed to enjoying independent, professional life-styles; so, before their two children were born, they arranged to share the responsibilities for child care equally. After the children were born, Nancy continued to pursue her successful career as a lawyer, while Marvin's work in journalism gave him a sufficiently flexible schedule so that he could either provide child care or supervise the paid child care and domestic services they needed when they could not be at home.

In spite of their many work and family demands and pressures, Marvin and Nancy were able to maintain a relatively peaceful and meaningful home life. Their children clearly benefit from their parents' strengths, competencies, and high level of professional satisfaction. All family members cooperate to forge new ways of coping with, and even enjoying, their demanding challenges.

* * *

Lenny and Tina married when they were very young, and they had four small children before they were 25 years old. Tina works as a secretary, and Lenny drives a taxi. Lenny's autonomy allows him to modify his work responsibilities according to their family needs more easily than Tina. They enrolled their children in a small day care center close to their home. Although this provision consumes a large portion of their combined income, they are pleased with the quality of supervision at the day care center. The peace of mind both Lenny and Tina attain as a result of making this practical arrangement more than offsets their concerns about the potential financial burden.

Lenny and Tina respect each other a great deal, and they amicably share childcare and housework tasks according to their own particular strengths and areas of expertise. Although the division of labor in their home still tends to be fairly traditional, Lenny assumes the responsibility of shopping and cooking for the whole family while Tina takes care of the laundry. Lenny and Tina share the housecleaning when necessary, and they both place a much higher priority on giving the children more attention than on completing household chores.

FAMILY INFLUENCES

Even though immeasurable disparities exist among families according to social class, ethnic group, culture, country, and historical setting, there are vital and enduring similarities among different kinds of families (Turner, 1970). We are all members of the human race, who need as much emotional support, meaning, and fulfillment as we can get from our families (von Bertalanffy, 1968).

This handbook suggests ways to solve family dilemmas that would otherwise limit our freedom. The strategies described are based on two facts: we have more potential than we generally use, and we express ourselves more fully when we are able to interact responsibly, yet autonomously, with our relatives.

New Families: Reviving and Creating Meaningful Bonds shows us specific ways to use our emotional resources and imaginations to improve the quality of our family relationships as well as increase the degree of cooperativeness among our relatives. Our goals to live constructively are achieved when we act decisively on our most nurturing ideals and ideas. Thus we create optimal living conditions for ourselves and others rather than further violence, competition, and greed.

Unless we pay attention to how we relate to our families and how they relate to us, we can easily become unwitting victims of emotional intensities we do not fully understand and cannot control. Because these strong influences have lethal properties, it is in our own interests to know as much as we can about our family interdependencies. This way we may avoid any negative consequences.

In many respects our families are sufficiently powerful to either facilitate or impede our functioning and fulfillment. Relatives' views of us influence how we see ourselves, and our self-images precipitate much of our behavior as well as our most cherished values and goals. Many aspects of our freedom are also defined through our families, or taken away by them. Only when we work toward creating new, freer families can we truly benefit from their support. Overly dependent families, whether they are traditional or nuclear in form, inevitably smother us and extend our immaturities.

Families are the most significant and deep sources of our ideals, . moral standards, and beliefs about reality. When we are sufficiently advantaged to know a considerable amount about our family histories, this knowledge enables us to understand ourselves better. Through our family histories we can more clearly see some of the patterns of values in our heritage and in our current daily lives. With these enriching objectives in mind, constructing a family history soon becomes a rewarding and ongoing task which is never complete.

Participating in our major family events and crises strengthens us and increases our capacity to claim our freedom both within and from our families. When we learn more details about our families and give our strengths to family members where needed, we belong more fully and more meaningfully to ourselves.

Whatever form a family takes–one-parent, adoptive, remarried, reconstituted, or other–the many patterns of emotional dependency among members remain more or less consistent. Our sexual and marital statuses do not define who we are as much as does our functioning within our family emotional systems. Paradoxically, when we can cope responsibly with others' claims, we can simultaneously move toward our own individual goals and ideals more effectively. If we are able to participate resourcefully during our family crises, we automatically create opportunities to become who we really are.

The work we need to do to become more firmly established in our own families is not necessarily all serious business. We can grow a great deal from having fun with our family ties. Devising a variety of ways to contact our relatives requires improvisation and ingenuity, and we can choose to organize some of our leisure time around innovative, enjoyable ways to visit and get to know "lost" or unknown relatives.

In a more serious vein, we must recognize that death in our families shows us how to understand the continuities in the lives of our relatives more fully and clearly. Consequences of aging and the passage of time are crucial aspects of the rich heritage that elders pass on to the young. We make sure we benefit from these special qualities when we participate directly in our relatives' aging and death.

Making our wills–a difficult and emotional task–is also a valuable learning experience, especially when we examine the wills of our deceased relatives. Wills are clear, shorthand messages about family members' values and affections. We understand ourselves more fully, within the context of the given complexity of our families' emotional systems, when we see what and where the most significant dependency patterns are (and were).

In spite of pressure to increase knowledge of our families, we are entitled to find much joy and satisfaction in our families. We cultivate such positive feelings more easily and effectively when we learn to say no as well as yes to our relatives, and when we interact with family members on our terms rather than theirs. By maintaining meaningful contact with our relatives, we establish effective means of coping with such crises as death, divorce, and dashed hopes. In order to be fulfilled, we must know how to meet our own needs and create our own delights. Our interdependence and family relatedness give us particularly significant clues about how to do this.

In order to build a "new" family, a family which will withstand multiple social pressures and persist through time, we must, to some degree, continuously focus on our family relationships. Constructive, flexible family bonding will reduce, or even neutralize, tensions that could otherwise become disruptive or destructive. Strengthening family bonds, as well as using specific creative or preventive strategies to keep family emotional systems open, effectively eliminate pressures and strains on new families and their individual members' lives.

When we know how to live well in the present, we are in a strong position to pass the torch on meaningfully to younger family members, and to let them know what our lives are really like. Families are a primary means to attain our goals of living freely and acting productively with others. What we do in our families prepares us for life in the world at large.

New Families: Reviving and Creating Meaningful Bonds directs us on an odyssey to find the deepest parts of ourselves. Although we still have to deal with the many blocks that exist in our traditional or nuclear families, if we move in the direction of creating new families, our lives will inevitably be increasingly fulfilled.

Chapter 2

Setting

To discuss specific current patterns of our changing families in the United States, we must first delineate some of the broader social trends and shifts that have occurred in the last few decades. Throughout this century, with ever-rising rates of divorce, U.S. families have become increasingly splintered and fragmented (Dizard & Gadlin, 1990). Lower birth rates have increased these segmenting tendencies. At the same time, other social institutions such as religion, which previously supported family functions and purposes, have become less effective in their family maintenance activities (D'Antonio & Aldous, 1983).

Although most life-expectancy rates have increased across the board by approximately 20 years since the turn of the century, some obstinately low rates persist among non-mainstream racial and ethnic groups and lower social classes (Levitan et al., 1988; Johnson, 1988). In addition to these baseline data, many researchers and clinicians predict continued breakdowns in the structures and processes we usually call family traditions (Popenoe, 1988).

In spite of well-documented increases in our everyday family stresses and problems, U.S. public policy has not yet been sufficiently well-formulated and well-organized to effectively minimize, or even reduce, their negative consequences for individual families and society. In many respects we have fallen short of several basic survival goals–goals already realized by Sweden and other European countries through legislated family support programs (A.C. Carlson, 1990).

The existence of contrasting lifestyles and relationship modes in the United States has forced us to broaden our definitions of families (Bagarozzi & Anderson, 1989; Milardo, 1988). Also, family variants among different ethnic groups show us myriad possibilities for family life in the United States and elsewhere (Mindel, Habenstein & Wright, 1988). Our awareness of these cultural contrasts inevitably expands our understanding of families and makes us question our assumptions about families and human nature (Mills, 1959).

However, some of the richly detailed findings from cross-cultural research also suggest that many similar patterns of communication, marital distress, and family violence exist in contrasting cultural contexts (Halford, Hahlweg, & Dunne, 1990; Levinson, 1989). These data help us gain a broader perspective on our own lives and a more objective view of our families. In these ways we come to more fully appreciate our families for what they are, thereby allowing our knowledge of facts to close the gap between our ideals and social realities (Pleck, 1987).

WOMEN AND MEN

During the 1970s, the second wave of feminism in the United States introduced more egalitarian values into mainstream, male-dominated society. As women slowly assume increasingly important positions in public life, they become more able and more likely to have an impact on history and institutionalized social class arrangements (C. Carlson, 1990).

Due to the complex nature of our interdependence as human beings, increases in women's independence have simultaneously changed the established, traditional relationships between women and men (Dornbusch & Strober, 1988). The new families that emerge in the midst of these fairly widespread adaptations are moving toward replacing previous hierarchies of male dominance with increasingly symmetrical relationship systems between women and men. For example, where both parents are present, new families are characterized by two heads rather than one.

Although feminism has by no means transformed all our families–in fact, many families continue to resist the impact of these egalitarian changes–we are now at least prompted to ask deeper questions about the real nature of our families and their gender arrangements (Ferree, 1990). In order to survive and raise our children responsibly, we must necessarily put aside some of our most traditional assumptions and perspectives. We need to more fully realize the positive and constructive support that new families bring to all their members.

Hard-won gains in family life satisfaction, especially those won by women, are not achieved without straining traditional roles and expectations (Galambos & Silbereisen, 1989). Although some relationship patterns are clearly changing to become more egalitarian (White, 1989), even through peaceful accommodation, many others stubbornly persist as male-dominated hierarchies (Finley, 1989). For example, many women who work outside the home are pressured to assume the double burden of their paid work and unpaid domestic responsibilities. These enforced tasks inhibit women, and may ultimately cripple their abilities (Zavella, 1987; Small & Riley, 1990).

TRANSITIONS

Although ethnic differences create rich diversification in family lifestyles (Thomas & Cornwall, 1990; Hampton, 1987; Waugh, Abu-Laban & Qureshi, 1991), most families share the role of primary emotional and social context for transmitting values to their members (Luster, Rhoades, & Haas, 1989). Families are also characterized by both the potential for violence and the propensity for gentleness (Gelles & Cornell, 1990; Hutchings, 1988; Russell, 1988). These contradictory qualities increase the difficulty of formulating policies to deal effectively with families' varied emotional tones and range of behaviors (Cherlin, 1988).

As our family needs cannot be met solely from within our families, we must be able to negotiate for the assistance we need for our families to both survive and thrive. For example, the provision of childcare by outside agencies is becoming an increasingly important need in a society with two-income families as its norm (Nelson, 1990).

New families have been able to strengthen their emotional resources and functional abilities through expansion of social networks (Milardo, 1988). As they increase their rootedness in society, they automatically benefit from local community agencies which may include significant institutional supports such as religion and education (Thomas & Cornwall, 1990). In this way, new families' strengthened bonds with society, and with extended family members, neutralize or even eliminate the frailties that are characteristic of most traditional or nuclear families (Dizard & Gadlin, 1990; Levitan et al., 1988).

HOPES AND REALITIES

To avoid falling prey to negative consequences that result from building up false hopes about our families, we must assess our family facts realistically (Halford, Hahlweg, & Dunne, 1990; Levinson, 1989). Generally speaking, families are not as unique as we like to believe they are (Mindel, Habenstein & Wright, 1988; Beal & Hochman, 1991). Many trends and patterns repeat through the life cycle (C. Carlson, 1990). Even revitalized new families show characteristics that have existed in one form or another for many generations in the same families (Dornbusch & Strober, 1988).

Given the increasing complexity of our families, it is essential to collect sufficient pertinent and accurate information about them. We can then increase our understanding and become able to formulate reliable and responsible strategies for crisis intervention (Pleck, 1987; C. Carlson, 1990; Cherlin, 1988). Although institutional supports such as religion inevitably have some impact on the quality of our family lives (D'Antonio et al., 1983; Thomas & Cornwall, 1990; Waugh et al., 1991), we must be able to build new families that reflect our highest values in their own right (Luster, Rhoades, & Haas, 1989) rather than endure families that express our most base qualities (Gelles & Cornell, 1990).

Feminism can move us toward creating new families that foster constructive growth for all members. This is because feminism prompts value changes which enhance tolerance and respect within families, and which help us adjust to stresses in our necessarily changing circumstances (C. Carlson, 1990; Dornbusch & Strober, 1988; Ferree, 1990). When women and men know and accept each other as equals, the mutual respect necessary for each person's achievement and fulfillment is present.

CHOICES

To deal effectively with these broader trends in society, we must make educated choices about which values and behaviors are most central to our own interests, and which meet the needs of our families, especially our children. We are not products of social influences, and we cannot completely determine our own life chances. We have to accurately discern what we can realistically choose, and therefore change, as we respond to the relentlessness of continuously shifting everyday situations (Mead, 1934; Mills, 1959).

The following list of choices suggests the kinds of freedom we must seize to strengthen our bonds with our families, and to strengthen our families themselves. New families are not necessarily defined by kinship ties, but they must have sufficient connectedness and depth in their relationships so that both personal self-realizations and broader contributions to society are attainable.

1. We must choose to live deliberately rather than automatically succumbing to our social conditioning, wherever and however we received that conditioning.
2. We must choose to recognize and respect the fact that everyone is different, with corresponding needs, and that we can only truly be ourselves when we know how to give to others.
3. When we choose to live fully, rather than partially and reactively, we must necessarily map out new directions for ourselves. Our changed behavior will inevitably challenge or upset the values and cherished traditions of those who are closest to us emotionally. However, these predictable negative responses, which will be accompanied by pressure to return to previous behaviors, must not deter our quest to live fully and be true to ourselves. Compromise and capitulation are not in our long-term interests, and they are not in the long-term interests of our families.
4. When we choose to focus only on our differences–race, sex, ethnicity, or religion, for example–we easily miss seeing and appreciating the many ways in which we are alike. Once we have identified our social location through our differences, it is important to move on with our lives, acting as much as pos-

sible as though there were no differences. Only when we are
sufficiently courageous to claim for ourselves what we want to
give to others are we really able to live fully.

5. By choosing to see the broader picture of our lives, and by
   simultaneously refusing to be victims or even willing recipi-
   ents of pernicious social influences, we can more objectively
   assess who we are and how we wish to relate to others. Our
   families provide us with our most accurate and most meaningful context for seeing ourselves as we really are, and for interacting with others about matters of substance.

6. When we choose to see the social and emotional dimensions
   of who we are in relation to our families, and society at large,
   we will be able to formulate appropriate questions to ask ourselves and others, and to realize their answers. We must
   choose discovery of these realities and claim them if we are to
   accomplish our hearts' desires.

Chapter 3

Questions

Before we examine specific family influences that strongly affect our lives, it will be useful to consider a few basic questions about families. These questions will be answered, at least in part, by the discussions and presentations in this book.

As a starting point, and to understand what some of our new families' strengths and possibilities are, we must identify ways in which our families characteristically free or restrict us (Bengtson, 1975). Although we prefer to believe that we will experience only positive influences when we live in close quarters with our families, very frequently the reverse may be true.

All families have both functional and dysfunctional aspects (Falicov, 1988). Even during crises, some parts of the family may function extremely effectively, no matter how stressful those problem conditions (Jackson, 1968a). By examining families that survive and thrive despite various stresses, we can ascertain how individuals and families change from passively adapting to external pressures to actively engaging in cooperative participation. This change ultimately minimizes or neutralizes their conflicts (Pfeifer & Sussman, 1991).

Research on the patterns of helping behavior in families suggests that families continue to be the primary source of values and sustenance for the majority of the U.S. population (Sussman, 1953; Slater, 1970; McGoldrick, Pearce & Giordano, 1982). Even though it is difficult to formulate watertight theories that measure the actual strength of specific family influences on individual behavior (Toman, 1976; Sprey, 1988), we can justifiably consider families to be among our most significant mediating influences and structures in society (Mills, 1959; Morris, 1967; Keniston, 1965; Christiansen,

1964). Even in modern, highly industrialized societies, family norms exert strong controls and establish significant worldviews for most people (Adams, 1968; Zurcher, 1983).

At the interpersonal level, as well as the broad societal level, family connections usually make or break our emotional well-being and life satisfaction (Jackson, 1968b; Caplan, 1989). Deepening our understanding of our own families is generally one of our most meaningful achievements. To accomplish this, we must first become aware of subtle dimensions of our interdependence. A wide range of dependency patterns are represented, suggested, or confronted by the following questions.

HOW DO NEW FAMILIES WORK WELL TOGETHER?

We need to know the qualities and structures of our new families–those characteristics which enable new families to survive and thrive despite adversity, or even because of it–in order to understand how members cooperate and coordinate their activities. Specifically, we must ask whether our new families are hierarchical or symmetrical, and then observe what impact new family structures have on the ways in which members interact.

What is it about negotiations and exchanges between new family members that creates satisfying working relations? If new family members are considered different but equal, can this kind of openness establish optimal conditions for both individuals and families?

What stages do new families go through when they deal effectively with crises and transitions? Can the degree of cooperation among new families' members of different generations be assessed accurately?

WHAT CAN WE DO TO INCREASE OUR ABILITY TO ACT CONSTRUCTIVELY IN OUR FAMILIES?

In order to answer this question, we need to know to what extent self-awareness and individual orientation toward constructive goals increase our capacity to contribute to our families. How do the unique interdependence and emotional reactivity of our everyday family transactions (which result from our lifetime membership and intergenerational bonds) support or impede our actions? Due to families' qualitative difference from other small groups and social institutions, we need to know effective ways to interact within them and to deal directly with our emotional connectedness to other family members. Does knowing ourselves in relation to our families, and having specific constructive goals to accomplish, increase our ability to act constructively?

By heightening our awareness of ourselves and our values, especially in relation to other family members, will we make our actions in our families more effective and worthwhile? Self-knowledge is not easy to attain. Frequently it entails discovering the history of our most significant family relationships, including those of past generations as well as our own lifetimes.

WHAT ARE OUR INDIVIDUAL AND FAMILY RESPONSIBILITIES?

Is defining our individual and family responsibilities a moral or a behavioral issue? Clinicians and researchers suggest that certain consequences flow from particular decisions and behavior. In this respect, empirical data can inform our moral decisions and make us more accountable for the consequences of our actions, thereby increasing our level of responsibility.

Do members of new families assume more responsibility for their behavior than members of traditional and nuclear families? How can women and men cultivate sufficient respect for each other to proceed toward their most meaningful goals, at the same time allowing others to do the same? Do families with mutual respect have fewer problems and less symptomatic behavior than other families?

How can we gain confidence from our family connections? Does being goal-directed, compassionate, and respectful toward others generate or nurture confidence? What are the advantages of being active with respect to our families? How can we stay in meaningful contact with family members on all generational levels during our everyday transactions and negotiations?

In pressure situations, does choosing to accept our own responsibilities enable others to fulfill themselves? Is some tension between individual and social responsibilities inevitable? When individuals act responsibly, do patterns of family interaction typically become constructive and supportive rather than divided with respect to the interests of the whole family? Does cooperative give-and-take which characterizes new families flow directly from the sum total of responsible individual actions?

HOW CAN WOMEN AND MEN GET ALONG PRODUCTIVELY WITHIN FAMILIES?

Are women and men who assume flexible gender roles more able to cooperate productively with each other than those whose lives are dictated more by cultural stereotypes? Do women and men who polarize their personal characteristics and lifestyles, and who romanticize human nature according to traditional gender stereotypes, inevitably set themselves up for emotional let-downs and more lasting disappointments?

To what extent is give-and-take the essence of interaction within new families? Is symmetrical reciprocity between women and men as constructive as negotiations which primarily give meaning and support to each other? Can any kind of dominance or subordination by either sex meet their own and others' long-term interests? How do power imbalances between women and men skew their relationships and affect personal growth?

How can both women and men be challenged to overcome the cultural stereotypes that dictate their lifestyles? In what specific respects do sexual stereotypes diminish the quality of our lives? How can we discover our own uniqueness and deliberately value it above others' gender definitions? What does it take to survive sanely and be fulfilled?

WHAT PREDICTABLE FAMILY CONFLICTS MUST WE FACE?

How do births, marriages, and deaths bring about crises in family relationships and changes in our worldviews? When we make efforts to establish our own individuality and identity, are we inevitably faced with significant others' negative demands, needs, and expectations? Does a new family become more immune to these pressures by encouraging its members to fulfill their own responsibilities before meeting the needs of others? Is being responsive to our own needs selfish, or are we only able to help others effectively when we have taken care of our own needs first?

Do we typically receive pressure to return to our former behavior whenever we try to do things differently in our families? Do new families have fewer resistant reactions among relatives when all or many family members try to become more independent? Are reactions within new families potentially conflictual in the same way that conflicts are predictable and almost impossible to avoid in most kinds of family interaction? Is it advantageous to anticipate conflicts when we take measures to grow and develop? How can we learn to deal with conflicts constructively and know when it is necessary to do this?

Due to the unavoidability of some degree of conflict, is it accurate or realistic to see conflict in positive rather than negative terms? Can we avoid being destroyed, or even threatened, by family conflicts? How can we make ourselves see conflict more productively-that is, as a source of growth and change, and as evidence that we are bringing about constructive change in our family emotional systems?

WHAT SATISFACTIONS AND FULFILLMENTS CAN OUR FAMILIES GIVE US?

Can families give us security even though they may be unloving and unsupportive? Is it true that we are who we are, and nothing can take away our innate characteristics? Can we understand ourselves more fully through examining and researching our family connections? Does self-understanding generate satisfaction and fulfillment in other areas of our lives?

Are families more supportive when we *allow* family members to be themselves, or when we *demand* that they be themselves? Does it follow that unless we take strength from our families our family resources will atrophy and disappear? Can only we claim our family heritages of durable connections and values? How can we make our own families work for us in order to be fulfilled? Do our families need us to need them in order to function effectively for all members?

HOW CAN WE GIVE THE MOST TO OUR FAMILIES?

What does giving to our families really mean? Is reciprocity the essence of sound family relationships? How can we sufficiently control our behavior so that we can give voluntarily and productively to our families?

What is it that our families need us to give? Does individual responsibility directly concern or take into account other family members' behavior? Does the quality of our giving to others inevitably result from our past or present family dependencies? What can we do to make our contributions to our families more constructive?

Does our most essential gift to our families consist of being responsive to family crises, or being responsible for our own growth and development? Is our giving truly independent, or is our behavior strongly influenced by others? Do those who are most dependent on us benefit directly from our interaction with other family members?

HOW WILL NEW FAMILIES SURVIVE INTO THE FUTURE?

What is the evidence that new families survive more effectively than traditional or nuclear families? Do single-parent and reconstituted families have strengths that traditional or nuclear families do not? How are family emotional systems perpetuated?

What characteristics of family interaction lead to family survival? Can those families that break down and become extinct contribute to social welfare or individual well-being as they disintegrate? Is individual variability within and among families so great that valid generalizations cannot be made?

Can families survive in their own right, or are they ultimately inextricably dependent on other social institutions (such as the economy) for their existence? Can individual family members contribute substantially to their families' capacity to survive? What advantages can we gain from new families? Why is it worthwhile to try to create a new family?

SUMMARY

These are some of the questions we need to ask in an age when families appear to be breaking down. We need to discover whether the new families that are surviving and thriving can give us qualitatively different views of family potential and benefits.

Some of the answers to these basic questions will result from reflection as well as planned action within our own families. As most of us have observed family exchanges at close quarters, we are aware of some of the advantages and disadvantages they can offer for our own growth and development. We need to understand why it is so difficult for families to survive modern social pressures and simultaneously maintain meaningful bonds. Our surviving, thriving new families are sources of valuable information that can benefit us all.

Chapter 4

Why Care About Our Families?

From an evolutionary perspective, families are the oldest human groups. They have been necessary for our survival since the earliest developmental stages of Homo sapiens (Darwin, 1964; Morris, 1967; Wilson, 1980). One implication of this fact is that contemporary families must be resilient enough to last indefinitely if we are to continue to exist rather than become extinct (Goode, 1963; Farber, 1973; Bengtson, 1975).

Due to our need to depend on viable families for our survival, it is reasonable to assume that most of the constant flux and manifold transitions seen in contemporary families are our attempts to effectively adapt to rapid social changes. For example, members' varied efforts to respond constructively to modern technological environments, and to each others' needs and adaptations, suggest that traditional family forms no longer meet our basic survival needs (Skolnick & Skolnick, 1989; Dahrendorf, 1959; Eggebeen & Uhlenberg, 1985).

Even in our current state of family instability, we cannot escape the fact that, to some extent, we are all products of our families–or are strongly influenced by those who played and continue to play the most crucial emotional roles in our early and recent development (Freud, 1958; Cooley, 1964; de Beauvoir, 1974). Even if we choose to live in complete or partial violation of much of what our original families taught us, our families are still our primary sources of being and behavior (Blau, 1964; Dinnerstein, 1977; Falicov, 1988).

With the increasing complexity of family forms, our own families may not remotely resemble the trim nuclear units of parents and children which have characterized the United States and other modern industrial societies throughout this century (Saxton, 1990; Clavan, 1978). Given the wide range of possible families, we may be, for example, members of a tightly knit but fragmented nuclear family, members of a large "organic" kin group, or members of a formally defined family of emotionally unavailable and geographically distant individuals (Wirth, 1931; Staples, 1986).

Whatever the variation of family forms we experience, our deepest roots are found in our families of origin (Ackerman, 1970; Sprey, 1988). It is a formidable advantage to feel securely but flexibly attached to our families amidst the many speedy technological shifts of modern civilization (Baltes & Brim, 1980). Families are essentially the only personal, intimate groups that have survived rapid industrialization, impersonal bureaucratization, and "disenchanting" secularization. We gain strength and perspective when we recognize that both our primitive and sophisticated selves derive from the same powerful family sources and influences (Kreppner & Lerner, 1989).

One of the most valid reasons to pay attention to our families is that if we take them for granted or ignore them, we will be increasingly likely to become their victims (Jackson, 1968a). Unless we know who our relatives really are, and what they do with their lives and ours, we can spend decades being pushed or pulled in directions we did not really choose for ourselves (Bowen, 1978).

This view of our families' potential destructive powers is realistic rather than negative or pessimistic. If we are to survive and live fully, seeing some of the dangers that can result from neglecting our families helps us avoid these same dangers. It does not matter how we become interested in valuing our families, as long as we recognize this urgency for us to know and come to terms with the wide variety of rhythms and patterns that our families perpetuate in our daily lives (Kluckhohn & Strodtbeck, 1961).

NEGATIVE REASONS TO CARE ABOUT OUR FAMILIES

A few negative consequences may convince us it is in our own interests to take our families seriously, and to care about how we interact with them. Such reasons incorporate the following considerations:

1. If we do manage to completely escape from our families or push them away temporarily—which is not easily done—they

will inevitably perpetually haunt us. The everlasting presence and influence of our families are felt at extremely deep, sometimes hidden, levels of our experiences. Although we cannot possibly get rid of our families, we can neutralize some of their influence by understanding them. We are free when we persist in interacting with our families maturely, rather than try to retreat from them.

2. When we merely rebel against our families, we remain forever tied to them through our own reactive behavior. Constantly taking positions against our families is an emotional slavery we need to consciously abolish.

3. If we do not examine ourselves carefully in the context of our families, we will not be able to get to know ourselves adequately. Consequently we will not be able to fully take charge of our lives. We only really know ourselves when we understand these intensely emotional sources of our conditioning.

4. Our children are prevented from repeating destructive family patterns only when we effectively interrupt, neutralize, or reverse these same processes. Unless we deliberately take direct action to stop negative intergenerational repetition of behavior in our families, these patterns will eventually automatically define our own children's behavior.

5. If we understand ourselves from the point of view of our functioning position within our families, we will come to know ourselves more fully in other situations. Our families are representative microcosms of society. What we are able to accomplish in our families enhances our contributions to diverse social groups, although the reverse does not necessarily hold true: we cannot always adequately exercise social skills we learn from other social situations in the emotionally intense environment of our families.

POSITIVE REASONS TO CARE ABOUT OUR FAMILIES

Though it may not be easy to see positive reasons to care about our families, the following advantages do exist. In some respects, these positive reasons extend or exceed the negative reasons outlined, and some are constructive goals in their own right.

1. Deep meaning derives from experiencing continuities in our lives (Levinson, 1978). Our families link us directly to both general and specific pasts; their relationship systems provide us with feasible ways to make these emotional and intellectual connections effectively. Personal histories, genealogies, and regional studies provide us with some of our richest perspectives for living fully in the present.

2. Families support us, even though both we and our relatives may fail to recognize that our exchanges and interactions are protective (Durkheim, 1951). The fact that we have a family, or significant others (including all kinds of family substitutes or alternatives), means that we are not alone in the world, that we have a group with which to identify closely, and that we are therefore less vulnerable to the strains and stresses of everyday living.

3. Many people count on their families to be there for them when they make major life changes (Bellah et al., 1985). Families have the emotional tenacity to persist through the most dramatic changes their members may make whereas, by contrast, even the best of friends may disappear overnight when a friendship is sufficiently stressed. Our families will not necessarily approve of our behavior, but they exist and continue to exist whatever we do. Our right to claim our lifetime membership in our families also persists. This means that we can rightfully continue to claim our privileges of family membership, even if our relatives cut us off or reject us. Thus, we cannot be fully excluded by our families unless *we* allow that to happen.

4. Our family histories give us vital information about our own socialization, and they show us who we really are in the present (Jackson, 1968b). We understand ourselves and our heritage more fully and more accurately when we closely examine patterns of behavior that existed in past generations of our families.

5. We gain emotional freedom when we establish ourselves and who we are–our identities–in direct relation to our families.

We prepare ourselves for more effective participation in the world at large when we take independent stands with respect to our family members.

WHO ARE OUR FAMILIES?

Families are groups whose lifetime membership is defined by kinship or legal contract (Engels, 1955). Families are also emotional systems. Although other small groups may also be thought of as emotional systems (Homans, 1961), especially family substitutes or alternative families, it is usually nuclear rather than extended families that are our most intense emotional systems.

When membership in alternative families lasts for a lifetime, the characteristics of these groups become more similar to those of kin-based families. The most important differences between family alternatives and kin-based families are that alternatives (1) frequently do not perpetuate their bonds with deceased members and (2) generally do not have the equivalent of past generations in their groups.

If you want to research your family, but find it difficult to locate or know who your relatives are, initiate contacts with as many of your family members as you can find as a critical first stage of your project. This strategy will give you additional information about your family while broadening your base of emotional connections. Your new contacts with an increased number of relatives provide you with a meaningful and secure context for your already established family relationships, and for all your other behavior.

Some guidelines for increasing your connectedness with peripheral family members are listed below:

- Make your goal the creation of an extended family network which will not disintegrate easily.
- Locate fragments of your family, and consider all these isolated relatives as mainstream family members in your thoughts, plans, and acts concerning your family.
- Get to know those who were closest to both you and your parents when you and they were young. Claim them for your

own, whether or not they are still alive, and whether or not they want to be claimed.

CARING FOR OUR FAMILIES

Romantic ideas about our families imply that we should love our families unconditionally. This ideal is difficult for most of us to understand or define, let alone achieve.

In order to be realistic, we must be open to the idea that love and concern can be expressed in many different ways. We need not be sweetness and light to one and all in order to be loving or caring. In fact, it is essential that we be resilient when we love our relatives so that we may deal effectively with intimate relationship issues, and with all the potentially lethal qualities of our family emotional systems.

There are ways we can and must protect ourselves at the same time that we must continue to love and respect our families. If we manage to give strong and hardy love to our relatives, we ourselves are strengthened through this interactive process.

Some suggestions for cultivating a healthy, interdependent, and mutually supportive love for your family and relatives are outlined here:

– Observe all your family members closely. Know where you stand in relation to them, and know where they think they stand in relation to you. Do what has to be done in family exchanges, and no more (unless you have your own particular reasons to do so). Do not let relationship concerns obfuscate your individual priorities. Get into the habit of interacting with your family members on your terms, not theirs.
– Love your relatives with some reserve, but care fully about what it is that you say and do with them. Behave sincerely and authentically, but do not try to do only what your relatives expect or want you to do.
– Do not automatically please your family before yourself. Know who you are and what you want at all times. Make your own goals your first priority, but pay attention to what other family

members need in order to fulfill themselves. Try to give your relatives constructive support whenever it is feasible to do so.

VARIATIONS IN FAMILIES

In order to envision what your family could be, it is helpful to consider what some of the optimal conditions of family life are. Families that encourage their members to be all that they can be are clearly preferable to those that restrict or inhibit their members' behaviors.

One way to begin formulating a clear picture of what kind of family you want to have is to recognize destructive behavior in your family. The examples given here illustrate some contrasts between detrimental and constructive family processes.

Negative Family Patterns

Susan left home at the age of 17 and did not return to visit her family during her adult years. She married and had three children, but she sustained little contact with her relatives.

Susan's estrangement from her family origins fueled her overinvolvement with her husband and children. Within 10 years her marriage broke up because of the intensity of her dependency on her husband. In addition to this crisis, her children developed problems in school and in the local community.

Susan's relatively "rootless" existence triggered emotional consequences that prevented her and her immediate family from functioning adequately. Her lack of emotional maturity intensified her nuclear family's emotional system so much that rupture and dysfunction were the only ways her family members were able to deal with each other.

*   *   *

Richard married a woman his parents did not like, and he decided to move several thousands of miles away from his family. His estrangement from his parents, and his two children's lack of contact with these grandparents, gave Richard's nuclear family less emotional support than it needed.

Although Richard's marriage survived the emotional intensity generated within his own family, his relationship with his wife became distant and meaningless. Richard's children were not healthy and required much medical care at high financial cost. These stresses further intensified emotions in this nuclear family and made it increasingly difficult for members to function adequately.

Positive Family Patterns

Both Helen's parents died when she was a teenager. She lived with her aunt, her mother's sister, during the last few years she spent in her hometown before going to college.

In spite of having no parents, Helen decided to learn as much as she could about her parents' families, getting to know her parents better through their surviving relatives. She contacted family members she had not even known existed during her parents' lifetimes, and spent some of her vacations and holidays with them.

Within a few years, Helen had essentially created a new family for herself. She was a happy young woman and performed well in college and graduate school. She maintained close ties with her family after she married and had her own children.

* * *

Mark had frequently disagreed with his parents for as long as he could remember. However, he fought constructively with them, and forged considerable independence for himself by differing from them over this extended period of time.

Mark matured at a young age. He selected a career he passionately wanted to pursue rather than following his parents' wishes and expectations. He studied poetry rather than medicine as his father had done before him, and as both his parents had hoped he would.

Mark continued to consistently express his differences with

his parents in mature and constructive ways which went far beyond mere rebellion. In spite of disagreeing with his parents, he genuinely respected many of their values and goals. This further enabled him to develop his own strengths quickly and effectively.

POINTS TO REMEMBER

Before reading further about possibilities for creating new families, and for making your own family work more effectively for you and your relatives, examine and affirm your orientation to your family by considering applying some of the strategies listed below. These pointers are designed to suggest directions that will ultimately free you from your most restrictive family dependencies. Paradoxically, the means to accomplishing this emotional liberation will lead you directly into your most inhibiting family situations.

1. Pay attention to your family, and see what is really going on during everyday exchanges and on special occasions. Realize that if you do not exercise such vigilance, there will be unintended but predictable penalties for both you and your children.
2. Find ways to continue your relationships with close family members, no matter how strained these relationships may be. Be willing to tolerate uncomfortable feelings in order to develop relationships with relatives you might otherwise prefer to ignore or leave behind. The benefits of establishing these new family bonds far outweigh those short-term disadvantages. You will accomplish this most effectively by finding or creating reasons to interact with as many of your relatives as possible, whatever your "natural" rapport with them may be, and by consistently aiming to increase the meaningfulness of your exchanges with them.
3. Continuously carve out your freedom for yourself within your family, utilizing unceasing and unflagging efforts. Seize your freedom by interacting directly with your relatives rather than retreating from them.
4. Discover as many detailed facts as possible about your family

history. Get to know who your relatives are and were, and what they do and did with their lives. Develop specific strategies to record all the information you collect about your family: keep systematic notes on family facts; draw family trees to define and clarify different relationships between your relatives; map patterns of closeness, conflict, and other qualities of relationships among your family members. Keep the present–as well as the past–in focus throughout your research.

5. Be deliberate about what you say and do with your relatives. Refuse to be a victim of family pressures, and refuse to be pushed to do what you do not want to do.

Chapter 5

Do Our Families Care About Us?

People who believe they already have a happy family life generally consider the question of whether their families really care about them to be redundant, inappropriate, or even offensive. In reality, many of us are essentially clinging to deeply cherished myths (a "family romance") that dictate that our families unqualifiedly do or should love us, rather than facing essential facts about our families and their behavior (Ackerman, 1958).

From an evolutionary perspective, our families need us every bit as much as we need them, to survive and endure through complex, rapid, technological changes (Parsons & Bales, 1955). These family needs may be so powerful that families are compelled to pull members back into their relationship systems in times of crisis, rather than allow them to move outward and onward with their lives (Koos, 1973). The enmeshment of individual and family needs is so complete that when we are pushed to excel, and we respond by achieving specific goals, the direction and momentum we claim as our own may actually be the result of meeting family needs (Frazier, 1939).

The degree of caring manifested in families is neither determined nor necessarily strongly affected by a family's access to material resources (Minuchin, 1974). Many over-caring and under-caring families are prosperous, whereas some of the most balanced, open, and supportive families are disadvantaged (Hanscombe & Forster, 1982). Because many patterns of family interaction cross social class and ethnic group boundaries, family interdependence and reactivity can be described as a levelling human experience.

Family intensities affect us all a great deal, frequently more than we realize. Whatever our social class, ethnic group, religion, or national origin, families are basic sources of our values and conditioning. Families orient us to the world and frequently define our most important goals. As emotional needs and family dependency are universal (Guerin, 1976), some family characteristics cross class, ethnic group, religious, and national boundaries. A family's style of caring is essentially a product of its emotional system; when we know what our families' emotional systems are like, we will understand our families and ourselves more fully (Dunn, 1985).

CONTRASTS IN CARING

One basic dilemma of the human condition is that everyone needs some caring and attention–not too much and not too little–in order to survive and live fully (Steinmetz, 1988). In light of this fact, some families should stop caring so much about each other, while other families should express themselves more freely and give more attention to their members.

Human beings are necessarily interdependent, and this inclination toward dependency can be seen most clearly through family relationships (Minuchin & Fishman, 1981). As a result, we tend to stay under the influence of our families, at least to some extent, throughout our lives (Baruch & Barnett, 1983). This means that what our families think of us remains important to us, whether we choose to accept or reject our own families' values. Even though we are able to neutralize or eliminate some of the stereotypes and images that our families construct about us, this task requires exhaustive efforts which may effectively limit our freedom.

Three family types are described below in order to illustrate contrasting styles of attentiveness: the family that cares too much; the family that cares too little; and the family that cares just the right amount. These influences affect our emotional tone and motivation, as well as the goals we choose in our everyday and long-term decision making.

The Family That Cares Too Much

All immediate family members are deeply involved with each other in this kind of family. Everyone knows everyone else's business, and there is an excess of shared intimacy and intense feelings. Those who choose not to conform to family expectations find it difficult to be accepted by their relatives.

There is little contact with distant relatives in these families, as the innermost circle of family members is tightly restricted and relatively impervious to outside contacts. This family emotional system is characterized by a great deal of gossip, praise, and blame, as well as by many secrets and taboos.

The Family That Cares Too Little

Unspoken, unexpressed emotion permeates the atmosphere of this kind of family, and outward appearances suggest distance and disinterest among these family members. However, there are strong feelings underlying the apparent lack of involvement, and the very intensity of this undercurrent creates alienation and estrangement.

These families frequently have a great deal of geographic separation (physical distance is often correlated with emotional distance). Although feelings are not readily expressed in these families, there are several predictable periodic or dramatic outbursts of emotions, as well as unexpected negative incidents and accidents.

The Family That Cares Just Right

This kind of family, which is characteristic of a new family, creates the healthiest emotional environment for its members; that is, an ambience that allows them to grow and thrive. Exchanges include the clear and direct expression of feelings, with relatively few outbursts of destructive emotions.

Members of these families lead comparatively well-balanced lives. They are mature and autonomous, and interact freely within both their nuclear and extended family emotional systems. They are also able to really be themselves; they are more concerned with pursuing their own goals than with testing degrees of commitment within their personal relationships.

Families that care just the right amount meet their members' emotional needs by accepting, supporting, and understanding them. Relatives respect, or at least tolerate, each other and do not engage in repetitive, unproductive conflicts.

FULL LIVING

Most of us want to live fully. In order to accomplish this effectively, we must relate to our families in balanced ways (Lynn, 1974). For example, we need to show up for family events and everyday routines rather than run away or retreat. At the same time we must avoid overinvolvement with particular family members (Gross, 1985).

Steering clear of overconcern for those who are near and dear to us is not easy (Chodorow, 1978). However, in order to live productively, we must allow ourselves and others to move freely inside and outside our relationships. Ideally, family bonds are elastic and life-supporting rather than tight, rigid, or restrictive.

Full living also results from giving to others. When we simultaneously meet our own needs and make meaningful contributions to other family members, we bring our intake and output with respect to our family emotional systems into a favorable balance.

As a consequence of living fully, we parent more effectively. When our own actions are positive examples for our children and grandchildren, we gain lasting satisfaction (Bengtson & Robertson, 1985). Our actions need to express life-giving messages to our families because our words are not as strong an influence on others' lives as our behavior.

WAKING UP

The emotional climate of our families is more than a context or background for our lives. The dominant shared feelings create a critical atmosphere, and serve as an effective starting point for our search to know who we are and what we want to do with our lives. The emotional intensity of our families establishes the quality of the springboard we can use to launch ourselves into the world (Colleta & Lee, 1983).

Seeing our families for who they are and what they are frees us from conventional myths and stereotypes. We cannot afford to be motivated or propelled solely by romance or resentment, as these emotions inevitably take us in directions that are not really our own and that may ultimately destroy us or others. We have to wake up to what may appear to be the harsh realities of our families so that we can prevent our dominant illusions from causing permanent damage (de Beauvoir, 1974; Dinnerstein, 1977).

Whatever the degree or quality of caring our families give us, it is to our advantage to stay connected with them through as many viable relationships as possible (Dean et al., 1989). We benefit from contacting family members and building many different kinds of meaningful relationships, even with our emotionally and geographically distant relatives. Broadening the base of our family emotional system essentially opens it up or keeps it open, and this kind of expansiveness and openness serves to dilute its potentially dangerous intensity. We are more able to deal with the present and future when we know some of our past, as it is the past that gives us roots and a secure base from which to proceed (Elder & Clipp, 1988).

DEPENDENCY ISSUES

Our freedom flows from the ability to express our innate human dependencies maturely and meaningfully. Our families do not automatically give us this freedom; all too often they either extend or suppress our dependency. Only rarely do our families encourage us to express our dependency constructively.

Illustrations of contrasts in family dependency are sketched below. A family that cares too much is referred to as a "smother-love" family; a family that cares too little is referred to as an "empty" family; and a family that cares just the right amount is referred to as a "life-giving" family. These different family style descriptions show how each style can hurt or help us, with emphases on the dramatically different consequences for our well-being. Regardless of the particular emotional style, it is strategically beneficial to be able to accurately assess how our families care for us, and what they actually think about us.

Smother-Love Families

1. Children in smother-love families are not able to learn to make their own decisions effectively. They are overprotected and

need parental guidance in concerns that should optimally be resolved by their own independent choices. Adults in these families also manifest the same immature patterns and tendencies.

2. People-pleasing is believed to be a supreme virtue for all members of a smother-love family, most especially for children.

3. Goal-setting abilities are inhibited or distorted by emotionally intense demands for love and other kinds of attention in smother-love families.

4. Deviations from family expectations are treated negatively in smother-love families, as relatives make a concerted effort to suppress or repress behavior of which they do not approve. Members frequently create and maintain secrets, resulting in the rupture of some of their closest relationships.

Empty Families

1. Empty families have deep-seated, unexpressed conflicts. Although these family members seem emotionally distant from each other, in fact, intense feelings underlie their apparent estrangement.

2. Members of empty families show little overt concern for each other. These families are characterized by lack of ready support, invisibility of emotions, dearth of "honest" feelings, and absence of open discussions.

3. Histories of empty families reveal rifts, unresolved disputes, and ongoing unproductive conflicts. Empty family "insiders" have rigid, negative attitudes about "outsiders," and there is little contact between these family members and other people.

4. Family relations are disrupted by a wide range of family problems that appear to be unconnected, and yet are reciprocally related. Severe behavior problems tend to erupt unpredictably and unexplainably in empty families.

Life-Giving Families

1. The highest shared priority in life-giving families–and a characteristic of new families–is individual freedom. Family mem-

bers receive support for being who they are or who they want to be. Concern and respect for each other are expressed directly and openly.

2. Because members of life-giving families are able to move either toward or away from each other easily, they are able to achieve their own goals effectively in the outside world.

3. Members of life-giving families communicate clearly with each other through behavior as well as words. There is sometimes a "tough love" tone to the orientation of members within these families, as all members are held equally responsible for their behavior.

4. Communications in life-giving families are consistent. Members are able to integrate their emotions, ideas, and actions during their exchanges with each other and with outsiders.

CONSEQUENCES

Whatever kind of family we are from, we open up our family emotional systems and create new families when we deliberately make constructive changes in our communications and interactions. Openness is achieved through responsible behavior that takes others' reactions into account, and through giving close attention to the consequences of our own actions.

We resolve nothing by leaving our families, unless their conditions are extraordinarily hostile or life threatening. Even in this situation, returning to our families (or at least to some members of our extended families) can ultimately be beneficial. Staying in meaningful touch with as many family members as possible has benefits for all members of the same emotional system.

New families are those that stay connected to each other and have flexible roles, especially gender roles. Their emotional tone is balanced and unblocked by either too much or too little caring. Autonomy is the main prize to be sought in all families, whatever the kind of caring our family emotional systems may give us.

Chapter 6

Who Defines Who We Are?

"Who am I?" is one of the most fundamental questions we can ask ourselves (Cooley, 1964). "Who am I?" is also one of the easiest questions to ignore–even for a lifetime–or answer simplistically (Blumer, 1969).

All too often, we take our human nature and our identity for granted, without any questioning whatsoever (Gerth & Mills, 1953). Or we think that they are immutable (Garfinkel, 1967). If we ask other people who we are, they usually tell us how they see us or, more accurately, how they want to see us. When we are undecided about how we see ourselves, we are too ready to accept who others say we are as our essence (Dally, 1982).

The definitions of ourselves that we accept have powerful consequences in our lives (Wentworth, 1980). The definitions of ourselves that we accept from others generally have strong negative consequences for us, even though these definitions may originate from family members who are emotionally closest to us (Toman, 1976). Our parents are our most influential definers, but other family members' views may also have a strong impact on us, depending on these members' closeness or importance to us (Rossi & Rossi, 1990).

EARLY IMPRESSIONS

When we are young, our elders watch us play and interact with our peers. It is usually these elders' memories, not ours, that structure our first impressions of the world, our family histories, and our views of who we were and are. We become a picture, story, or myth–a collage of others' views and beliefs about us (Straus, 1979).

Although others' impressions of us are essentially fictitious, as we become adults we must learn how to cope with significant others' beliefs about who we are. It takes a long time, and much deliberate attention and energy, to debunk others' positive and negative personal mythologies about us (Leonard, 1983). Only when we stand firmly on the ground of who we really are can we claim our freedom through our personal relationships.

Family emotional processes would be less important in our lives if others' memories and convictions were not as powerful (Lynn, 1974). Relatives' impressions all too easily become facts in our lives, and we are frequently unable to discern whether certain past events and behavior did or did not happen (Kivett, 1985). Did we really do the things we were supposed to have done? To what extent do we live our lives through others' imaginations?

SEPARATING FACT FROM FICTION

In order to be fully responsible for our behavior, we need to establish the most significant facts in our lives and discover who we really are (Kinsey, Pomeroy, & Martin, 1948 and 1953). Ideally, this sorting-out process culminates in the construction of accurate family histories (Hill et al., 1970).

The first stages of our research should pinpoint the most pertinent facts that affect us now, as well as those facts that have affected us most strongly in the past. This task usually requires talking with as many family members as possible to become more objective about the past and present. The more views of ourselves and our relatives we can collect from insider family members, the more objectively we can define who we are and where we are in the midst of our own powerful emotional dependencies (Glass, Bengtson, & Dunham, 1986).

To go beyond any family illusions, we must be able to see through distortions of reality (Goffman, 1959). Recording basic facts about births, marriages, and deaths is one effective level of inquiry; discovering family secrets, hypocrisies, and lies is another viable approach (Hurvitz, 1979). As we make progress, we become more able to see which of our family bonds are strongest (i.e., those which have been repeated and perpetuated over several generations) and to locate gaps in family connectedness (i.e., where no one has information, or where no one is willing to give the facts).

Our quest to find our true selves necessarily leads directly into the densest centers of our families' confusions and mutual pressures (Mann, 1988). These emotional vortexes are our most powerful, vital origins. If we want sufficient freedom to create and pursue our own goals, we must first know something about our social sources (Durkheim, 1951).

SOURCE

Our families can be thought of as both real and metaphorical sources of our being (Straus, 1984). All families have both dysfunctional and functional characteristics, but none of these patterns need have sufficient impact to determine who we are. When we are in charge of our lives, we are who we are in spite of our families (Levinson, 1978).

We must review and consider as many facts as possible about past generations in order to thoroughly examine and understand our families. Our family values and ideals are perpetuated by patterns of emotional intensity in relationships through successive generations (Merton & Kitt, 1969). Who were the religious leaders in our families? Who were atheists? Who was indifferent? These kinds of questions and issues are important to resolve, as information about the emotional tone of our families helps us know more about our own functional positions in the complex mass of family exchanges, and explains–at least partially–how we have come to think and feel about ourselves and our lives as we do (Parsons, 1968).

Early in our upbringing we are taught or conditioned to have certain ideas and ideals (Rosenberg & Kaplan, 1982). Who and what are the exact sources of these ideas? Our ideas and ideals pervade our lives and strongly influence the level of our education, the kind of occupations we follow, and our aspirations for the good life. Most of all, our dominant self-concepts strongly determine our everyday behavior and transactions (Stryker, 1968).

Our most central idea of who we are originates as a consequence of the particular patterns in our family dependencies, ideals, and expectations. In this respect, our journeys to our real selves are necessarily informed by our family values. It is up to us to decide whether we want to keep our families' ideals and expectations as our own, thus agreeing to accept and perpetuate them, or whether we prefer to claim alternative values (Lee, 1955).

IDENTITY

All the values we learn and absorb unconsciously from our families necessarily become or affect the core of our being (Berger & Luckmann, 1966; Gilligan, 1982; Gerth & Mills, 1946). Although we may eventually choose to modify these values, our initial programming is inevitably a basic foundation of our selves. This programming derives directly from the values and beliefs of our original most-significant others (Arcana, 1986; Benson, 1968). As our behavior flows directly from who we think we are, it is imperative that we decide, through our current decisions and activities, what values and what kind of lives we want to identify with (Fein, 1988).

Through examining our exchanges within two- and three-person family relationships, we can find out much about who we are, as well as ways in which our beliefs and decisions create our identities from the values we have or want to have (Berger & Kellner, 1977). Characteristic dynamics of these dyadic and triadic units also represent and magnify how we typically behave with people outside our families (Boszormenyi-Nagy & Framo, 1965). For example, our participation in the dyads and triads of our families' interaction patterns shows us whether we are habitually dominant, subservient, dependent, detached, or egalitarian in our exchanges. These characteristic patterns tend to be repeated in other social settings (Cohler & Grunebaum, 1981; Fischer, 1981 and 1986; Boyd, 1989).

Even though any research we do on our self-development by creating family histories necessarily emphasizes the past, we essentially collect this information for current purposes. We cannot avoid giving due consideration to the past if we are to function effectively in the present and future (de Beauvoir, 1974; Dinnerstein, 1977). Ideally our past should be used as the most practical orientation for our current circumstances, in that our knowledge of our past allows us to deal with the present and the future more constructively and with greater awareness of our own strengths and weaknesses (Elder

& Clipp, 1988). Ultimately, however, our past is not as directly significant to our functioning and well-being as our present and future.

Family histories help us formulate effective strategies for living in the present and future. Knowledge of the facts about who we are and where we came from at the outset of our journeys toward self-discovery and self-realization is a sound, irreplaceable advantage. The more knowledgeable we are about who we are, the more successful our personal growth is likely to be (Chess & Thomas, 1986).

We must persist in building awareness of our self-definitions because these particular ideas and ideals have powerful behavioral and social outcomes. All of our everyday activities flow from, or are influenced by, our identities–who we know ourselves to be and who we believe we are.

It is in these respects that our most influential self-fulfilling prophecies are our knowledge and beliefs about ourselves. The expectations and actions from varied aspects of our lives derive from our self-definitions. Because family messages tend to persist at the core of our original identities, these value influences have the potential of lasting a lifetime (Kassop, 1987). We must decisively accept or replace our family values with our own values if we want to be autonomous; that is, to be free in our own right and on our own terms (Hanson & Bozett, 1985).

IDENTITIES IN THE REAL WORLD

Two examples illustrate how definitions of self and identity influence behavior. Contrasts between Peter's and Jennifer's experiences suggest a range of possible kinds of identity, together with their related behavioral outcomes.

> Peter does not have a clearly defined identity, as he has not made any consistent and deliberate effort to understand who he is. His father died when he was seven years old, and his mother did not remarry or include many men in her life. Consequently, Peter found it difficult to learn or understand what was expected of him as a boy and man in the world beyond his family.

Peter's social contacts were narrowly restricted by his family circumstances. He has a younger brother and sister, and his mother frequently demanded that he look after them. This ongoing responsibility meant that Peter was not able to be playful or carefree during his childhood and adolescence.

Peter, his brother, sister, and mother live in geographic and emotional isolation from the rest of their family. As a conscientious and dutiful son, Peter developed a strong concern for his mother's well-being early in his life, and this filial posture and overly concerned attitude continue in his adulthood. Peter's preoccupation with his mother's needs results in his inability to understand who he really is.

At times Peter appears to be disoriented. Developmentally, he is behind his peers in making major decisions about an occupation or career to pursue, and he does not have many friends. Due to Peter's habitual indecisiveness about his education and social life, even as an adult he functions largely in reaction to his mother's needs as well as those of his younger brother and sister. He is unable to place sufficient priority on his own life to make effective decisions for himself.

*   *   *

Jennifer has a clear idea of who she is and what she wants to do with her life. She is the middle child of a family of seven. Her frequent disputes with her brothers and sisters helped her to know and express her own likes and dislikes from an early age.

Jennifer stays in meaningful contact with many members of her family, including several relatives of the older generations. She also willingly assists her parents when they need special attention.

Jennifer has decided to delay marriage in order to give herself sufficient time to develop her fledgling career in business. She is increasingly successful in the management position she holds with a large company in a nearby city.

Jennifer is constantly aware of who she is and what she wants when she interacts with her large family. She defines her own goals clearly and pursues them, especially her career aspirations, rather than acquiescing to what her parents or brothers and sisters think she should do. Although she is willing to cooperate and live peacefully with her family, she does not allow relatives to have an inordinate influence on her life.

TASKS FOR DEFINING YOUR IDENTITY

Several techniques can strengthen your functional position within your family. Your identification with specific values forms the core of your potential for effective behavior, and for the accomplishment of the goals you care most about. Modifying your deepest values has far-reaching effects on your actions.

1. Observe yourself to see when your strongest emotions are activated. Be particularly vigilant about noting times and situations when you feel the most anger or the most satisfaction.
2. Keep a record of current and past significant emotional events. Try to get an accurate overview of the major events or turning points that have occurred in your family, and note those that you think affected you the most.
3. Collaborate with other family members in the construction of a family history. Pay particular attention to how other same-sex relatives lived in previous generations. What occupations did they have? When did they marry? When did they have children? How many children did they have? Were they in good health? Did they travel? When did they die? How did they die?
4. Reflect on your values, and consciously identify with those values that have the most meaning for you, whatever your family's values may be.
5. Notice how your identity influences your behavior. See how you express your values in everyday exchanges with others, and how you make clearer communications and behave more effectively when you know what your values are.
6. When you make changes in your beliefs and behavior, a negative reaction from other family members, especially those who are emotionally closest to you, is predictable. Expect this resistance, and be prepared to withstand relatives' pressure to

change your behavior back to its previous form. Persist in your new directions while maintaining some meaningful contact with your relatives.

7. Make continuous efforts to clarify your identity, regardless of external circumstances. Identity empowerment is not a single event in your life, but a lifetime process. The rewards from undertaking this venture are inestimable.

Chapter 7

Family Histories

Family histories come in many different shapes and sizes. Completed histories may be bound in leather and gold or scribbled in a scratch pad. Some family histories are collections of audiotapes or videotapes. They may consist of items like interviews with older family members or records of special events like marriages. Family histories may also consist of collections of photographs of relatives and special family occasions, as well as pictures drawn by children and other family members.

These compilations are essentially maps of where specific groups of people are going, or diagrams of members' major gains and losses (Cohler & Grunebaum, 1981; Falicov, 1988). Both discovery and mystery are integral parts of family histories since it is usually extraordinarily difficult to get accurate personal information about relatives, especially if they have been dead for 50 years or more.

For the pragmatic purpose of creating bonds for a new family, every family member–those who are widely known as well as those who are relatively unknown–should be included in a family's history (Lee, 1980). An accurate and representative history cannot result from a selective coverage of relatives and their lifelines (Kingson, Hirshorn, & Cornman, 1986).

Making such a comprehensive effort to compose a family history generates large amounts of information. It is the breadth of the data and their context that will help make the finished product more objective (Mangen, Bengtson, & Landry, 1988). Only an extensive family history can adequately reflect the degree of subtle complexities and intricacies within the patterns of intergenerational exchanges (Adams, 1968).

ADVANTAGES OF COMPILING
YOUR FAMILY HISTORY

Before beginning to invest time and energy in an exhausting project of this kind–or to become sufficiently motivated to begin such a venture–it is helpful to review some advantages of creating and completing a family history.

1. A family history deepens and enriches your understanding of your heritage and your roots.
2. In your family history you will be able to see patterns between generations and within relationships that are not readily apparent, or even visible, in the everyday give-and-take of the present.
3. Lifespan data on all family members indicate the strongest and weakest parts of your family dependencies.
4. Seeing the extent to which your life duplicates others' past experiences gives you a valuable new perspective on yourself. It also helps prevent repetition of behavior you do not want to recur.
5. Making your family's past known can free you of some of those most insidious influences that would otherwise pervade the present. For example, making family secrets known can benefit the whole family when a release of information opens up the family's emotional system.
6. Family history seems to be an inherently interesting topic for the conversation and further research of all family members. Even though those relatives who have the most vested interest in the status quo will predictably resist your efforts to collect information, you will be able to easily engage others–including those who do not volunteer to help you with your project–in your continuing task of discovering facts. A family history is never finished, and its continuity can sustain members' curiosity over long periods of time, even over generations.
7. An important dividend of your effort to compile a family history is that you will invariably experience a stronger sense of belonging to your family. Whether through actually receiving and exchanging information, or through spending energy on traveling and studying official historical records, you will

necessarily become more rooted. Paradoxically, you will at the same time become freer.

INFORMANTS

For the purpose of compiling your family history, any family member is a potential informant. In reality, however, some relatives will not be sufficiently motivated to participate in gathering past facts and information. Some may even stalwartly resist your efforts by refusing to cooperate with you (Dunn, 1985). Initially, only the strongest and freest family members will encourage you and want to assist you in your research. This is because most people tend to automatically put aside the past, especially if it is disconcerting, rather than examine it (Mills, 1959; Goode, 1963).

Do not let your relatives' lack of enthusiasm for a family history daunt you in your quest. Rather, expect that at least some family members, including those who are emotionally closest to you, will be hostile as you pursue your research project (Glass, Bengtson, & Dunham, 1986). Do what you can to advance your task deliberately and calmly, without unnecessarily stirring up opposition.

Relatives on the periphery of your family are often surprisingly helpful and well-informed about other family members and significant family events. They themselves may have been ostracized by the majority of their relatives, or they may have cut themselves off from the family for reasons of their own. In spite of the relative isolation of such peripheral relatives, they frequently have a refreshingly different view of the family, as well as information that is not generally known.

Establishing meaningful contact with relatives who are perceived to be on the outside of the usual definitions of your family also gives you a unique connection with those family members you know very well. Most relatives are curious and relieved to learn about family members they do not know, or about those they do not frequently see or hear from.

RAW MATERIALS

Take whatever information you can get from your relatives as substance for building your family history. Sometimes the tallest stories and most pithy anecdotes you hear will have some truth to them or at least intrinsic interest because they are communicated by your relatives. Remember that all oral reports must be respected and considered seriously since these diverse stories comprise the life-blood of family histories.

Sometimes the same anecdotes are repeated by different family members. It is these repeated themes that can most help us check out what is real: this overlapping information allows us to increase both the objectivity and accuracy of our histories. Intentionally recounting the anecdotes you have been told to other relatives is not only an effective control for their veracity, but a personal communication that forges bonds where none might have existed before. As you collect and disseminate this kind of personal information, you will feel both more integrated with your family and freer from its controls.

Official documents such as records of births, marriages, and deaths, or wills, are invaluable guides to knowing a family's past (Pruitt, 1981). In order to retrieve information that goes beyond the memory and records of living family elders, you will need to do additional research in local libraries or offices where legal records are kept. If this kind of in-depth project is too overwhelming or too time consuming for you to undertake easily, and if you have sufficient means, paying for professional assistance from genealogical researchers can be invaluable.

SECRETS

Discreet uncovering and discussion of family secrets may be a particularly effective means of freeing up your family–and yourself–as you continue to compile your family history. The process of putting facts together reveals and demystifies many different kinds of family secrets. This debunking process releases their hold on you, and even on those who were not aware that the secrets existed.

Family secrets do not protect anyone, even though they may have been at least nominally instigated for this purpose. In fact, most family secrets may ultimately prove to be extremely hazardous for all family members (Bowen, 1978).

Repetition of negative behavior is especially likely to occur in families that have many secrets (that is, where facts about problematic situations are not widely known). Creating a family history puts information together in such a way that some revelation of secrets is inevitable. This process is beneficial, as it is these very revelations that decrease the likelihood of the occurrence of future negative events.

It is important to be cautious, kind, and diplomatic when you reveal a family secret. The act of divulging sensitive information necessarily brings risks, and irresponsible communications immediately precipitate negative consequences for the parties involved. Give yourself and the family members you are informing plenty of time to deal with the disclosed facts, as well as with the personal dimensions of the situation. Don't just make brief, business-like statements. Be sure to extend your presence and availability for assistance and discussion if needed when you know that the newly revealed information will be hurtful.

Sometimes family secrets are built around particular taboos. For example, there may be a conspiracy of silence about topics such as sexuality or death. Your own openness about these taboo subjects can decrease or eventually even break their power, but you should simultaneously expect negative reactions or resistance from those who actively sustain the taboos.

One related objective of acting in ways to neutralize the power of taboos is to dilute the power and emotional intensity wielded by family members who created the original rules and regulations which others now feel compelled to keep. Families become more alive and more flexible, as well as more open when these restrictions are minimized.

Dysfunctional families have more secrets than families that function well. Reducing the number and power of secrets in these families decreases their dysfunctions. In many respects, compiling a family history may realistically be thought of as an ongoing opportunity to discover and reveal family secrets. Interestingly enough, however, these constructive consequences result most frequently when the primary aim is to collect information and do research rather than dispel secrets.

AUTHORS

When you assume responsibility for compiling a family history, you become an author. In some ways these goal-directed activities also make you an authority on the family–at least as far as other family members are concerned.

There are many ways in which you can present yourself to your relatives as the author of your family's history. You may choose to circulate the complete edition, or partial versions of your finished product. Or, your history may be so raw and cumbersome that this is not possible.

In order to illustrate the range of possibilities for authoring a family history, two contrasting examples are given below. When deciding what your own style for researching family facts will be, reflect on how you work with others most effectively and what particular characteristics you think your family has.

> Graham used a relatively formal approach when he first started to collect information for his family history. In order to collect the most basic facts from his relatives he mailed out identical explanatory letters and questionnaires to all the family members he could locate.
>
> After Graham received some completed questionnaires, he used the information he collected about relatives he did not initially know to send them identical and subsequent mailings. Even though Graham's research style was fairly impersonal, he found that many of his "unknown" relatives responded cooperatively to his requests. In addition to completing his questionnaires, relatives expressed a surprisingly deep personal interest in knowing more about their family history.
>
> It was sometimes difficult for Graham to deal with the volume of information he received from his relatives, and he had to deal with frequent overlaps in his data. However, within a few months' time, he was able to compile a fairly orderly family history. He then mailed this to all his known relatives, whether or not they had participated in his project by sending him information.
>
> Graham continued his research beyond this first version of his family history. Fragments of information continued to be retrieved at later times, and increasing numbers of his relatives volunteered facts and figures for his records. Graham became known as the family historian, and family members tended to give him information whenever they saw him.

* * *

Hazel collected photographs as a starting point for her family history. She also recorded conversations she held with some of her older relatives. Her exchanges strengthened her bonds with the family members she contacted and interviewed, and some of them gave her the privilege of looking at wills of deceased relatives.

Although Hazel did not actually write a history of her family, she made her strong interests known by specific questions and requests for information about deceased relatives and past events. Members of her family came to count on her for this kind of knowledge. They also began to give her information about these matters without needing to request it.

Hazel felt personally enriched by this intensive effort to understand her family. She does not have children of her own, but young members of her family are strongly attracted to her because they feel her interest and concern. It is mainly because of her project that they see her as a well-informed, comforting person who gives them a sense of security. Hazel consistently has stories to tell them about their family.

WHERE TO GO FROM HERE

There is some danger, as well as a great deal of joy and satisfaction, in creating family histories. It is perilously easy to get stuck in the past, forever researching and rewriting your family history, without connecting the records with a living reality in the present. Remember that the most rewarding reasons for developing a family history are (1) to understand yourself and your most significant others more fully in the present, and (2) to provide guidance in articulating meaningful directions for your future (Toman, 1976). Keeping these more transcendent priorities in mind helps you make sense of endless details from the past and prevents them from suffocating or impeding you.

Family histories, however, are much more than background information or an orientation for the future (Hays & Mindel, 1973). Records of family events reflect past and present intensities in family emotional systems. They show patterns in the course a family has taken to the present, and they serve as predictions of possible continuities in the future (Lewis, 1982; Hill et al., 1970).

Your family history is an effective source or base for accomplishing self-realization through initiating and establishing new family connections (Johnson & Barer, 1987). In fact, your family history necessarily functions as a starting point or springboard for launching yourself into the real world (Parsons, 1951).

Whatever the richness of detail from the past, your research will eventually strengthen your motivation for achieving self-realization, in particular by enabling you to view both the present and the future more objectively and more honestly (Guerin, 1976). Your family history can dramatically move you further along on your journey toward living your life more fully in the present (Gilmour & Duck, 1986; Friedman, 1985).

Chapter 8

Keep Looking Ahead!

Family histories are reliable and vital sources of knowledge and know-how that can be used as orientation for present and future actions (Frazier, 1939). Collections of family facts made over long periods of time show patterns and tendencies in family strengths, weaknesses, problems, and achievements. Family histories serve as checks on the reality and viability of our present or future being and goals (Bernard, 1974).

Although our present objectives should ideally transcend what has already been accomplished by ourselves or our families, it is helpful to note the directions family members have taken before us (Hill et al., 1970). Records of what happened, and how, may also serve as an inspiration or guide for how things could be. The facts of our relatives' lives are valuable means to understand our potential, as well as to know the probabilities and possibilities of functioning or achieving specific goals (Glass, Bengtson, & Dunham, 1986; Lee & Ellithorpe, 1982).

When we know and respond constructively to the facts of our families' pasts, we are freer to be ourselves in the present and the future. If we recognize and know how powerful our own family emotional processes are, we can no longer be victimized by them (Johnson, 1982). However, in order to fully understand our families in this way, we must first see them through a time span of several generations (Pfeifer & Sussman, 1991). The more we take our families for granted, or deny the importance of their influence on our lives, the more they will dominate our selection of goals and relationships without either our intention or our awareness (Johnson, 1988).

PRACTICAL STEPS

One important behavioral principle says that we function more effectively when we know where we are, have our own goals, and know where we are going (Young & Wilmott, 1973). Several practical steps can be taken to implement this principle. Reviewing our pasts establishes our starting points, but our ideals and specific objectives sustain purpose and give future direction to our lives. In the final analysis, it is strategically more important for us to know where we are going than to merely recognize where we are, although optimally we should be aware of both locations (Farrell, 1974).

The following list suggests ways in which we can definitively move ahead in our lives without merely reacting or acting in preordained ways. These steps are not coordinated in a tightly systematized sequence, but rather describe a variety of substantially equal and significant forward moves.

1. We need the benefits that derive from attending and participating in our families' major events on our terms, which means that we must resist our inclinations to avoid major crises like births, marriages, and deaths. These happenings are significant turning points in our family histories. We learn a great deal about our own family emotional processes by observing others and participating with them at such openly reactive times. This valuable knowledge will clarify our directions for the future as well as yield additional vital information about our pasts.

2. We need to plan different strategies and specific ways to participate in our family routines so that we can be sure we do these on our own terms. Although our plans for our participation cannot be infallible, or perhaps even reliable, constructive and self-protective action might not take place unless it is carefully planned. In most circumstances it is much easier to retreat from family emotional systems than to interact with them directly. Given the nature and intensity of emotional processes and patterns of family interaction, unless we develop specific strategies for participating in crises

before their occurrence, we will inevitably distance ourselves from our families at these stressful times.

3. We can benefit from using knowledge of our family histories to contact little-known or unknown relatives. These newly initiated family relationships will not only be rewarding in their own right, but they will invariably improve our relationships with our parents and other central family members through expansion of our networks of emotional contacts. We must make sure these relationships stay as meaningful as possible by continuing to visit or interact with our newly acquainted relatives on our own terms.

4. It is worthwhile to get to know deceased family members more fully by contacting their relatives and friends, or by visiting places and organizations that meant a great deal to them during their lives. This investment of time and energy deepens our family roots, which in the long run enables us to move in freer and more meaningful future directions.

5. Getting to know younger family members by doing things with them, or by just spending time with them, is valuable. Telling young relatives about our lives and what our families are like benefits them as well as ourselves. These exchanges create and maintain bonds with them and enable us to indirectly influence the future development of our families.

6. Concentrating on our current options and decisions helps us build strong futures. Detailed knowledge of our families' pasts is useful only insofar as it can guide our present and future decision making.

7. Once we have sufficiently acknowledged and understood the power and influence of our families on our lives–past, present, and future–then we can further empower our identities by moving more decisively into community life. We gain emotional strength from our new family bonds, and as a result our views of the present and the future are more realistic and productive. The same emotional strength also allows us to transcend our current problems and difficulties.

8. When we have children, we must parent loosely in order to give them the freedom they need to grow in their own ways. We must try not to burden them needlessly with our own

hopes and expectations. If there are problems in our families, we must first examine our own behavior closely to see how we may be contributing to these difficulties, and correct our behavior where necessary. We must not automatically blame our children for family problems, but rather relate the difficulties we may experience to our overall family processes.

9. We sustain our efforts to move effectively into the future by giving our full attention to our own goals. We cannot afford to shift our focuses to relationships, because we lose sight of our objectives when we become overly engrossed in interpersonal concerns.

10. We need to examine our beliefs and identify which ones restrict our behavior most of all. When we have accomplished this, we must do our best to understand where and how our limiting beliefs developed and then discard them–or replace them with more constructive beliefs.

AUTONOMY

Our ability to be autonomous strengthens the effectiveness of our participation in present activities (Gilligan, 1982). We take charge of our lives and live fully when we are fully in control of our own time and energy.

To some extent we neutralize others' power over our behavior by adhering to our own goals which transcend their claims and expectations (Bloomfield, 1983; Lynn, 1974). In order to orient our action decisively toward the future at the same time that we express our deepest values, we must concentrate selectively on the goals we want most to accomplish (Mann, 1988).

Whatever our family form–single, married, divorced, or remarried–the question of which direction we want to go in must be answered as objectively and as honestly as possible. These goals should be articulated without direct reference to family status, since it is objectives rather than relationships that are crucial to our autonomy. When we review the facts of our lives and examine the roots of our family histories, we will predictably find clues to meaningful directions of accomplishment. We are able to maintain autonomy successfully when we keep these goals as our highest priorities rather than the quality of our family relationships (Madanes, 1981). However, at the same time that we work toward achieving our most cherished goals, the quality of our family relationships will also automatically improve.

When past family business has been taken care of, we can move into our futures more smoothly (Gross, 1985). To develop our potential, we must question–and, if necessary, change–our learned gender and sibling behavior rather than reactively meet others' needs, demands, and wishes (Fischer, 1981). This process helps us claim our freedom from our families and function more fully.

We gain our greatest security when we face the future from the vantage points of our family bases. We must anchor our personal relationships by activating connections to members of past generations while going beyond family structures to formulate and accomplish the goals we want most (Hoerning & Schaeffer, 1984).

CONTRASTING CONSEQUENCES

Three examples illustrate how we can orient ourselves to the future by acknowledging our ties to our families, and by focusing on goals we want to attain. Kathleen, Roger, and Wendy depend on their families in different ways. Their attitudes and future-oriented actions flow from their respective degrees of dependency.

Kathleen is relatively independent in her relationships with her family and, by contrast, Roger is markedly dependent. Wendy changes her customary behavior from dependent to independent, thus shifting her orientation toward the future. The descriptions show how family dependencies define who we think we are and what we think we are capable of doing.

Kathleen has a younger brother. She has been very aware of behavior patterns in her family since her mother's death, when Kathleen was only seven years old. Kathleen was raised by her aunt (her mother's younger sister) as well as her father, and she has had numerous contacts with members of her mother's family since her mother's death.

Kathleen recovered remarkably well from the loss of her mother. She quickly became accustomed to seeking out whatever support she needs from her distant relatives as well as those family members who are emotionally close to her. She benefitted a great deal from these varied connections. As a result, she was able to choose a meaningful career for herself and launch herself into independent adulthood. In these significant respects, Kathleen orients her everyday behavior to the future very effectively. She continues to depend on her family sufficiently to meet most of her emotional needs.

*   *   *

Roger has eight brothers and sisters. He was born in the middle of the time span between his oldest sister and youngest brother. He found it difficult to clearly define himself throughout his childhood. As an adult, Roger still does not know what he wants to do with his life. He does not like to compete with his brothers and sisters, but he finds that he needs their approval in order to function effectively.

In many ways Roger is even closer to his father than to his brothers and sisters. He is consistently anxious to please his father, and imitates him a great deal. Roger is slow to develop any autonomy or individuality with respect to his father or his siblings.

Roger decided to work in the family business. His extreme dependency on his family means that he constantly looks to his relatives for guidance in decision making. He continues to be oriented primarily to the outside world by the family values he absorbed and reinforced through his lifelong adaptive behavior.

Roger has great difficulty developing any vision or goals for his future. He is usually either immobilized by his family dependency or reactive to other family members by imitating them or following their suggestions of what to do. As Roger is not able to think clearly for himself or sort out his own priorities, he is not able to get on with his life by acting in accordance with his own values, goals, and preferences.

*   *   *

Wendy was very close to her parents and older sister as she grew up. However, during her courtship and marriage, she became much more independent. Throughout this period she examined her life more closely and chose her own goals more carefully.

Wendy's shift from dependence on her parents and sister to independence meant that she was able to take charge of her own life more effectively than when she was younger. She no longer depended on her parents or her older sister to guide her or suggest goals. She made her own decisions about long-range objectives and plans. She also persisted in future-oriented behavior that she believed would eventually accomplish her goals. As Wendy continued to behave this way, she developed a strong sense of self and made additional constructive choices for her future.

We cannot afford to let our families take away or diminish what it is we really want to accomplish (Bengtson & Robertson, 1985). The freedom we claim from and within our families becomes the firmest foundation for other social freedoms (Gilmour & Duck, 1986). We envision our futures most wisely when we steadfastly connect with our family bases as our starting points. In order to accomplish this, however, it is also necessary to transcend our family needs and our family connections by making meaningful contributions to society at large (Iutcovich & Iutcovich, 1987).

It is our involvement with this wider social good that is ultimately our most freeing condition and our greatest life satisfaction. Our new families support and nurture us as we move toward the accomplishment of this end, but they should not be ends in and of themselves. Our raisons d'être are to know our families but, at the same time, to go beyond them in the service of others.

Chapter 9

Families in Crisis

Advantages develop from any family crisis that coexist with the more intensely felt disadvantages (Goode, 1956). Crises are turning points, or newly developed stages, in the radical reorganization of our families and our individual relationships with our families (Cherlin, 1981; Rubin, 1983).

None of us can escape our need to deal effectively with family crises indefinitely (Colleta & Lee, 1983; Rubin, 1976). Even events that are generally joyful, like the birth of a child, create stress and their own kinds of crises (Klein & Aldous, 1988). Whenever members are either added to or taken away from our families, there are major behavioral consequences for all family members (Koos, 1973; Pruitt, 1981).

FAMILY NEEDS

A family is a unique small group because of its lifetime membership through kinship or contract (Hays & Mindel, 1973). Easily observed intense interdependency among family members makes it particularly useful to view a family as an emotional system with its own specific needs (Bowen, 1978). Some of these functional requirements must be met satisfactorily if a family is to survive and thrive rather than become extinct (Kingson, Hirshorn, & Cornman, 1986). Descriptions of selected basic prerequisites are listed below:

1. A family needs a stable membership. The more family members there are throughout different generations, the more stable a family tends to be. However, if this larger kinship group

divides into clearly demarcated nuclear families, and if the smaller units tend to withdraw from the whole, the family's overall stability is jeopardized. Such fragmentation is greatest when young families cut themselves off, both emotionally and geographically, from older generations. Ideally, connections between the larger kin group and the nuclear units should be actively nurtured as well as–sometimes more than–those within each nuclear family.

2. A family needs some degree of emotional equilibrium. Family members function most freely and are more likely to achieve their potential when a family is calm. At the same time, however, an essential shared characteristic of families is that they frequently express a wide range of feelings. Although not all families demonstrate extreme emotional contrasts, both tender love and violent, life-threatening abuse may be expressed within relatively short periods of time in the same family. Because intense and volatile feelings threaten the status quo of a family's emotional system, a family must achieve some degree of balance if it is to persist or become viable and productive.

3. Families thrive most when there are meaningful emotional contacts among many of their members. If a broad kin group splinters into nuclear families and if there is virtually no contact among family members except within those nuclear units, the family as a whole may not survive. When one or more relatives become estranged, their families tend to reject them. Consequently, the estranged family members withdraw further from their broad kin systems. The quality of contact and relationship among all family members is therefore harmed. The increased isolation of the estranged relatives precipitates an automatic and stressful tightening of bonds among those who are still in contact, with these bonds becoming volatile and easily ruptured.

CRISES

The occurrence of a family crisis suggests that one or more of the family's basic needs are not being met (Hill, 1949; Maslow, 1976;

Homans, 1961). A temporary crisis, however, such as unexpected disruptive events at the time of a birth, may typically be but a brief transitional period of emotional turmoil with no lasting negative consequences (Skolnick & Skolnick, 1989; Madanes, 1981).

In fact, families have ways and means of overcoming any kind of crisis (Liebow, 1966). Increased bonding frequently occurs, as many family members tend to support each other more than usual when difficult conditions exist (Stack, 1974; Johnson & Barer, 1987; Kivett, 1985; Lewis & Sussman, 1986).

Crises may be thought of as unusually intense patterns of family interaction which manifest themselves within a particular time sequence (Wallerstein & Kelly, 1980). Four crisis stages can be distinguished: initial conditions of tension or unrest; eruption of symptomatic behaviors; efforts to respond to the crisis and recuperate; and a resolution or chronic continuation of the crisis. These are essentially transitional stages in an overall adaptive process which aims to ensure that a family continues to exist and function well (Haley, 1976).

If we further apply such a broad longitudinal perspective, we can think of crises as series of events rather than isolated, fortuitous occurrences (Weitzman, 1985). Crises are particularly intense phases of family histories, when members live through dramas dictated by their own functional positions in the group (York, York, & Wachtel, 1982).

One benefit of crises is that, due to experiences of pain, family members become more receptive to possibilities for changing their problematic behavior (Glassner & Freedman, 1979; Iutcovich & Iutcovich, 1987; Hurvitz, 1979). Consequently, basic patterns of family interaction are modified more easily during crises than at other times (Gross, 1985; Steinmetz & Straus, 1974; Straus, Gelles, & Steinmetz, 1980).

Crises are inevitably important turning points in a family's history, whether or not therapeutic interventions are sought, and whether or not deliberate changes are made (Aldous, 1987; Anderson, 1984). Crises provide opportunities for immediate personal growth as well as resolution of long-term tensions created by members of past generations (Cicirelli, 1983).

RESPONSES TO CRISES

Since none of us can escape from the eventuality of crises, it is important to know how to deal with them when they do occur (Darwin, 1964; Garfinkel, 1967; Goody, 1962; Elder & Clipp, 1988; Caute, 1967). Some ways to respond constructively to family crises are suggested below. These instructions are intended to transform some aspects of family tragedies into opportunities for personal growth. They also may help resolve broader family tensions (Bettelheim, 1987; Gelfand & Barresi, 1987; Gil, 1970).

1. Stay calm and try to understand what is going on. Carefully note (either mentally or in writing) the essential facts as well as the characteristics of the attitudes and behaviors of key participants in the crisis. Stay as detached as possible from the emotional intensity of the crisis without being indifferent. Maintain meaningful contact with as many family members as possible throughout the different stages of the crisis.

2. Learn as much as you can about the history of problem conditions in your family. Give special attention to characteristics of present manifestations. Request information from those who are both directly and indirectly affected by the crisis. Pay more attention to the facts revealed by the situation than to the qualities of feelings expressed. Maintain the orientation of a researcher whenever possible. This posture will allow you to be more objective about the crisis experienced.

3. Keep moving along with activities in your own life. At the same time, avoid or refuse to be immobilized by the trauma. Be aware of all the decisions you make. Use a long-range perspective in your thinking and behavior whenever possible. Don't make immediate, short-range decisions and choices prompted by your anxiety or your perceived need to reduce tension in your family.

4. Take a stand on the painful issues when they arise, and maintain your stand whenever feasible. But be willing to make some adjustments, rather than rigidly adhering to your views at all costs. Your functional position results from your value choices and integrity, however, and your most important values will become non-negotiable at some point.

5. Move into the vortex of your family crisis rather than retreating from it. Given the predictable conditions of high anxiety during a crisis, it is generally easier to withdraw from these stresses than to participate in the core of intense family exchanges. However, it is by far to your advantage–for increased personal growth and effective long-range emotional resolutions within your family–to participate in at least some of the necessary confrontations in crisis situations. Solid personal growth occurs through challenges and exchanges with family members and significant others who do not abandon you easily.

6. Your presence during a crisis ensures that you can both learn from the situation and contribute constructively to other family members. In fact, it is only through deliberately cultivating an attitude of giving to others that you can eventually be fulfilled. Both you and your family lose opportunities for growth and resolution when you withdraw from a crisis.

7. As you "hang in there" and do what you can to respond to a family crisis you will become more free of relatives' routine claims and demands. Furthermore, family members remember how you acted when they needed you, and your constructive participation will bring the benefits of their increased respect. In this way, you will ultimately gain more independence from them.

8. Patterns of interaction during crises show that your family needs you. When you acknowledge the benefits you receive through contributing constructively to crises, you are able to more realistically identify the ways in which you, too, need your family. You cannot grow and mature as effectively by participating in other groups as you can by interacting with family members. This is due to the relative transitory nature of other groups. Even though family crises may appear and feel highly undesirable, they are crucibles in which people can grow and make profound positive change.

REACTIONS TO CRISES

In order to show some of the ways in which individuals respond to crises, three examples are given below: divorce, loss of a parent, and loss of a child. When the key participants in a crisis are able to act constructively, the family is able to create a particular mode of adaptation.

Divorce

Michael and Jean divorced after five years of marriage when Peter, their son, was two years old. Michael moved to an adjoining state and into an apartment in a small town, about 100 miles away from Jean and Peter. Jean received custody of Peter and continued to live in their family home.

Michael distanced himself from both Jean and Peter, and from the rest of his family. This rather extreme isolation hindered Michael's ability to adjust to his divorce, and he had difficulty concentrating on his work. He did not find his job in his new location interesting, and each day he disliked going to the office vehemently.

Jean was more successful than Michael in her attempts to adjust to her divorce. Several relatives lived in the same town, and with their assistance she was able to cope effectively with her daily needs and responsibilities. Jean spent many weekends with her family. Both she and Peter functioned well in spite of her underlying anger and strong sense of abandonment.

Jean soon found a job that paid well, and with some continuing help from her relatives, she was able to make adequate childcare arrangements for Peter. Both Jean and Peter thrived on their family supports and social contacts, and they soon settled into an uneventful but fairly well-balanced routine.

Death of a Parent

Harry was in his sixties when his mother died. He had lived 1,000 miles away from his mother most of his adult life. He was relatively uninvolved with her daily care even when she became ill and was dying. Two of Harry's sisters lived in his mother's home town, and he was relieved to leave her care in their hands.

Harry's characteristic pattern of emotional distance from his mother was duplicated in his interaction with his own nuclear family. He had been a relatively uninvolved parent while his children were growing up, and he continued to be essentially disinterested in their progress.

Although he would have undoubtedly found it extremely difficult to change his distant style of relating to his family at this late stage, he would have been able to make some behavioral modifications if he had chosen to play a more active role in his mother's health care, or in managing her affairs after her death. Because Harry did not respond constructively to these particular opportunities for change, the crisis of his mother's death did little more than perpetuate and accentuate his distance from his immediate family and sisters. After his mother died, Harry withdrew into an even more isolated position in his family, and in all his other social relationships.

By contrast, Harry's sisters became closer to their children during their mother's illness and death. Harry's sisters' children learned a great deal from watching their mothers participate in these crises, and they became more independent through their own experiences of their grandmother's death.

Death of a Child

Lilian had four children. She and her husband, Herbert, enjoyed parenting and family life, and their children did well in school. Their youngest child, Sam, was their most loved but most difficult child. Neither Lilian nor Herbert had wanted to limit their family to four children. So, when they were not able to have more children, Sam became their all-time favorite and shared emotional focus.

In spite of the special attention he received, or perhaps because of it, Sam became an accident-prone child at an early age. Sadly, he drowned in a boating accident when he was 13 years old, and all members of his family suffered a great deal from their tragic loss.

Lilian and Herbert grieved intensely for several years and could not come to terms with Sam's death. They became overly protective of their remaining children, with the result that these adolescents and young adults began to dysfunction and openly rebel against their parents.

The whole family became uncomfortably tight-knit after Sam's death. Lilian's and Herbert's pervasive, anxious concerns inhibited their children's normal growth and development. In addition to having overly cautious and possessive parenting styles and attitudes, Lilian and Herbert placed unreasonable pressure on their children to live up to impossible standards of family unity and agreement. This closure in their family emotional system meant that no family members were sufficiently free to express their real feelings, or to do what they most needed and wanted to do.

RESOLUTIONS

For optimal resolutions of crises, families must accept particular crises as ways to open up their relationships rather than as times to restrict their activities and the expression of their feelings (Dean et al., 1989; Furstenburg & Spanier, 1984). Personal advantages do not naturally or inevitably evolve from crises. Families must respond to crises in ways that provide conditions of openness rather than closure. These open conditions are necessary for the development of benefits (Stoller, 1983; Sussman, 1953).

Of the specific crisis scenarios described above, Jean made the most constructive adaptation to the chaos in her life as she dealt with her divorce. Her son, Peter, also benefitted directly from her newfound independence, while her husband, Michael, essentially retreated from his family and lost many opportunities to improve his functioning.

Harry's sisters experienced more personal growth from the death of their mother, as it was they who acted more supportively and more constructively when their mother became ill and died. His sisters' families also gained from the mature and considerate way in which his sisters responded to the losses of their mother's illness and death. His sisters' strengths were attractive examples for his sisters' children.

Lilian and Herbert were unable to cope with the death of their favorite and youngest son, Sam. Lilian's and Herbert's extreme grief essentially closed the family's emotional system after Sam's death. All family members were inhibited from expressing themselves adequately and from making any life-enhancing resolutions out of the loss.

PREPAREDNESS

At best, crises prepare us for the inevitable crises of the future, and for life itself. New families recognize and utilize opportunities that evolve from family exchanges during crises, so society itself ultimately benefits from the strengthening and opening up of particular families' emotional systems.

People generally do not grow and change unless they have real and meaningful reasons to do so. Clinical data suggest that change usually has no intrinsic interest for most people, unless they are uncomfortable or are suffering in some way (Angell, 1965). As a consequence, crises are great movers of change (Beal & Hochman, 1991). We decide to modify our attitudes and behavior only when our habits no longer work for us (Brody et al., 1989).

If one or two family members recognize that crises are not to be feared, and indeed may have beneficial consequences, relatives are gradually able to give each other the support and inspiration they need (Farber, 1973; McGoldrick, Pearce, & Giordano, 1982). Recognizing the importance and potential of families as emotional resources is a first stage in discovering some of the potential benefits of the crises that will occur throughout our lives (Slater, 1970; McAdoo, 1988).

Chapter 10

The Usual Kinds of Issues

Our families are frequently our most intimate, personal relationships (Skolnick & Skolnick, 1989). When we define families as those who are emotionally closest to us, we acknowledge that each family is an emotional system in its own right (Bowen, 1978). It matters relatively little whether the basis of our bonding with our own family members is biological, contractual, legal, or emotional. Both emotional closeness and distance can bond members to each other within the context of biological, contractual, legal, or emotional connections (Turner, 1970).

A family's status is ultimately less important for the well-being of its members than are family processes (Pruitt, 1981; Schur, 1971; Rubin, 1983). We are who we are largely due to the quality of our relationships and exchanges within our families (Shanas & Streib, 1965). If we want to make changes in our lives, these are the social bonds that are our most critical starting points (Christiansen, 1964). We must be able to open up our family emotional systems if we are to claim our freedom as women, men, gays, lesbians–whatever status we are ascribed or choose to claim (Colleta & Lee, 1983; Garfinkel, 1967; Goffman, 1959; Homans, 1961). New families are open family systems.

FAMILY STATUS AND FAMILY PROCESSES

To illustrate some of the connections that can be made between our functioning positions in our families, and the emotional processes that underlie intergenerational patterns of behavior and family exchanges, some different family statuses are listed below. The profiles given are general rather than specific, and therefore may seem impersonal. However, it is the same crude but basic patterns of family reactivity that need to be recognized and dealt with if we are to make successful adaptations and changes in our lives. These behaviors hold us in place, and in order to be free of them we must first see their restrictiveness (Iutcovich & Iutcovich, 1987; Haley, 1976). New families can only be cultivated when the restrictive ties of relatively closed family systems are seen and understood.

Biological Child

When we are born into families and maintain ties with those same families, the primary basis of our membership may be biological. We may have been born after a marriage, before a marriage, or without marriage. For emotional system purposes, it does not make a lasting difference what our legal status is. The emotional tone of the family we were born into has a much more significant influence on our lives than our legal status. The influence of the quality of the emotional bonds between our parents is so powerful that it establishes the tone for the whole family.

Some variation exists in the functioning positions of biological children with regard to their birth order and sex. The same family treats their children differently, but patterns of oldest, middle, and youngest children show similarities across social classes and ethnic groups, as do patterns in sex distribution and learned gender behavior among children.

Adopted Child

An adopted child's functioning position in a family emotional system is essentially the same as that of a biological child. Sometimes the circumstances surrounding an adoption are more intense than those surrounding a birth. For example, a child who is adopted by older parents after two decades of marriage, including several miscarriages, would probably have more emotional significance for those parents than a child who is born into a family after two years of marriage and no miscarriages. The status of adopted children and the quality of their development are much more intimately tied to their adoptive origins and family processes than to their biological parentage.

As with biological children, family size and sex distribution have a significant impact on the behavior of adopted children. The ranking of oldest, middle, or youngest child makes a difference in how adopted children are treated by their parents, brothers, and sisters, as well as the sex distribution and learned gender behavior typical of other members of those families. New families are able to interact with adopted children in the same ways that they interact or would interact with their own biological children.

Single Person

Most of us have families in the sense that we are usually raised by the same few individuals. Even singles who live alone continue to be someone's child, grandchild, brother, or sister.

A single person may also have many cousins, nephews, and nieces–or none. What is significant for understanding everyday behavior is that a single person has a status in both a nuclear family emotional system and an extended kin group. A single person cannot avoid participation in complex family processes, and in this respect singles are the same as married and divorced family members. A new family is able to recognize the advantages of these many diverse connections. Its active relationship system stretches beyond a procreative unit of parents and children to encompass the entire kin network.

Married Person

A married person has one of the most heavily socially sanctioned traditional statuses in a family. Marriage is a contract with legal, physiological, and emotional consequences for offspring of the union.

A married couple creates its own emotional system which inevitably includes all the children born into that marriage. Parents establish the emotional tone of a nuclear family, and they also participate in their own respective extended kin groups. Each parental kin group is a distinctively separate emotional system in its own right.

In new families, parental emotional systems are less intense and restrictive than in more conventional or traditional marriages.

Separated or Divorced Person

There are successful divorces as well as successful marriages. Divorced couples who have effectively terminated their marriages may closely resemble singles with respect to the quality of their participation in the emotional systems of their procreative and extended kin networks. However, to the extent that separated or divorced couples continue to be in very close contact or have emotionally volatile exchanges, their relationships will persistently resemble their marriages, emotionally, even after lengthy separations or long-completed divorces. Where there is a joint custody arrangement, divorced parents may interact even more intensely than some married parents.

Depending on the frequency of a divorced couple's interaction, and depending on the degree of reactivity during their exchanges, a couple's emotional bonds may not be significantly diminished by a divorce. Even in cases of severe emotional estrangement, geographical distance, alienation, and conflict, separated and divorced spouses generally retain at least some potential for continuing to be an extremely intense emotional system.

In new families, divorced persons are able to maintain some degree of contact in order to conduct their financial affairs and parenting arrangements civilly. Each former spouse is able to get on with living fully. These bonds and emotional systems are flexible and allow participants–and children–to come and go relatively freely.

Heterosexual Person

Generally there is little family or social concern about an individual who has a heterosexual orientation. Because most of the population is heterosexual, this is considered "normal." Where families or communities are homosexual, however, heterosexual outsiders may be ostracized or reacted to negatively because of their different or relative minority status.

When families are understood to be emotional systems, it is clear to see that one's sexual orientation does not matter as much as how other family members respond or react to that orientation. The less reactive heterosexuals are to homosexuality, the more viable a family emotional system will be. New families have this quality of responsiveness and flexibility.

Homosexual Person

When a family does not accept homosexuality, any gay or lesbian family member tends to be scapegoated or labelled a problem. When heterosexuality is the family norm and homosexuality is rejected, blame and criticism are predictably aimed at a homosexual family member. A homosexual orientation threatens the values and sense of legitimacy of some heterosexuals, even though heterosexuals are a statistical majority in the population at large.

Intense family reactivity to homosexuality is destructive for any family emotional system. The more closed a family emotional system is, the more negative its reaction to homosexuality will be. New families are able to accept their gay or lesbian members on their own terms, consequently their family emotional systems stay sufficiently open to allow freedom of action for gay, lesbian, or other family members.

Resistance to homosexuality is largely based on fear, and no particular family response is preordained. Most of our reactions are learned; their expression depends upon the specific circumstances as well as the degree of closure or openness of a particular family. Hostile or closed family processes can be changed to tolerate and accept homosexual members. In these respects, new families can evolve from even the most entrenched traditional family systems.

Transvestite Person

Although a person who is a transvestite may conventionally be considered deviant, their behavior will not precipitate negative reactions in the new family where most family members accept this behavior. A family's reactions to a transvestite member frequently depends on how deviant a transvestite is considered to be by that family. Sometimes particular social circumstances influence how family members see a transvestite. For example, a transvestite who has a successful job may tend to be more accepted by other family members than a transvestite who does not work.

The fact that society does not fully tolerate transvestites makes it more difficult for some families to accept their transvestite members. When transvestites are committed to being open about their lifestyles, family processes are more likely to eventually be changed to include them as equal participants when the behavior is hidden from others. Secrecy tightens family emotional systems and makes already existing negative reactivity more frequent and more intense; openness encourages more flexibility in family exchanges, which allows new families to develop.

Transsexual Person

When individual family members undergo surgery to change their biological sex, they may or may not be accepted by their families. It is the degree of openness in those family emotional systems, as well as the degree of determination of transsexual members to be themselves, that influences relatives to accept or reject those transsexual members. In a tolerant situation, which is characteristic of new families, a transsexual's unconventional decisions and behavior will not necessarily create any additional reactivity or intensity in that family's emotional system. New families deal effectively with wide ranges of behavior and allow all family members to interact with tolerance and respect for each other.

Parent

Although there are gender differences among the parental expectations and styles of different historical periods, cultures, classes, and ethnic groups, both parents have enduring responsibilities to raise their children creatively and constructively. Some parents fall far below established parental expectations, while others shoulder responsibilities that go beyond what any parents can be expected to do for their children.

One of the primary emotional responsibilities of parents is to interact with their children in consistent and balanced ways. This quality of participation in family emotional systems means that children and other family members will be more likely to function effectively in their own right than if a parent is overly zealous or overly responsible. In terms of meeting the basic needs of a family emotional system, being overly responsible is being irresponsible. New families are characterized by balanced parenting wherein each parent is able to pursue individual interests as well as subordinate some of those interests to child care needs.

Female

Traditionally, families are primary sites of women's oppression. In new families, there is an increasing recognition that male-dominated hierarchical authority structures are dysfunctional for all family members. A family emotional system that facilitates the equal participation of all members is much healthier and more viable than one in which adult male family members function at the expense of female and young male family members. New families are relatively egalitarian family emotional systems.

Special circumstances may serve to close or open family emotional systems, thereby making egalitarianism less or more possible. For example, families under stress frequently revert to established cultural patterns of male dominance. However, some of these tendencies are offset by contemporary increases in women's economic independence. When women are economically self-sufficient, their emotional independence is increased while their subordination is decreased. This chain of events is predictable, whatever the social class or ethnic group of the economically independent women. Gains in women's autonomy are not uniformly distributed in modern industrial societies, but there have been overall increases in women's independence throughout this century, especially with respect to the levels of women's subordination in past epochs. New families make women's autonomy more possible at home and in the workplace.

Male

Historically and culturally men have been more favored family members than women. However, in spite of these privileges, much family dysfunction and disruption has resulted from the relatively irresponsible behavior of men.

When trying to objectively distinguish characteristics of family emotional systems, it is more feasible to view men as potentially equal participants in a family emotional system than as the privileged or irresponsible family members they may actually be. Although all families are influenced by cultural norms, which tend to endorse the higher social status and greater power of men, when considering men's own long-range adaptations and viability, some degree of balance and equality within a family is necessary. Men's lifespans may be extended, for example, when men give more attention to their emotional needs than to cultural pressures to conform and perform in response to the conventional competitive male interests of society at large. In new families, more flexible gender definitions for men as well as women lead to greater autonomy and freedom, which is also shared by other family members.

FAMILY REACTIONS TO HOMOSEXUALITY

Two examples of family reactivity illustrate some of the power of these issues as bases of members' exchanges. Homosexuality may or may not be an emotionally taboo topic for any given family, but when family members react negatively upon learning that a relative is gay, especially an emotionally significant family member, the entire system becomes more closed through its interdependent reactivity. Only open and flexible family responses create conditions for the development of new families.

Ivan

Ivan is a 25-year-old single male, and the only child of Jane and Herbert. He is the apple of each parent's eye, and they have great expectations for his successful future as a lawyer. Ivan has already accomplished a great deal academically and professionally; his parents periodically try to further his precocious educational and career achievements by introducing him to some of their well-established friends in the local community.

Jane and Herbert were intensely shocked and upset to learn that Ivan was living with his college friend and lover, Lawrence. Ivan's parents had limited knowledge of what it meant to be homosexual, and this lifestyle seemed to them to be far removed from the conventionally ideal vision they cherished for their son's future.

In order to come to terms with their pain and embarrassment over Ivan's gay lifestyle, Jane and Herbert cut themselves off from their families and friends. They saw much less of Ivan than they had been accustomed to. Jane would not discuss her disappointment with Herbert, or with anyone else, and Herbert became depressed. Although Ivan proceeded with his homosexual lifestyle in the same way as before, he became very concerned about his parents' pain. He subsequently found that he and Lawrence tended to get into more fights than they had previously.

It was only when Ivan deliberately made contact with some of his relatives outside his nuclear family that the closure of his family emotional system was halted. Ivan did not keep his homosexuality secret. Although his parents were at first increasingly upset about his openness in telling relatives and friends about his personal life, in the long run Jane's and Herbert's families accepted Ivan and approached Jane and Herbert supportively.

Within a year, Ivan's family's emotional reactivity was transformed from relative closure to relative openness. Family members continued to accept Ivan's homosexuality as well as meet Jane's and Herbert's needs to be comforted and supported. Conditions for creating and sustaining a new family were brought into being, and all family members thrived from the increased flexibility in this family emotional system.

Diane

Diane came from a fairly large family where she was the oldest daughter of six children. Her father had died when she was a teenager, and she was routinely given much responsibility for helping raise her brothers and sisters.

When Diane started work in a local car manufacturing company, she found several close relationships with women who worked with her. While not having recognized any homosexual tendencies in earlier years, Diane now found herself sexually attracted to one of her co-workers, Mavis. Although Diane continued to live at home, and help out with her family's busy household, she developed a sexual liaison with Mavis and visited her frequently.

In order to accommodate her two very different lifestyles and expectations, Diane decided not to tell her family about her intimate relationship with Mavis. However, the intensity of her secrecy soon manifested itself as an undercurrent of uneasiness throughout her family. Even though Diane's relatives did not know exactly what was going on in her life, they all shared in the general malaise and anxiety that pervaded the family.

Diane herself was the most victimized by her secrecy and homosexual lifestyle. Her continued evasiveness further tightened the emotional reactivity in her nuclear family, and her fears of revelation affected her behavior and performance in many areas of her life. Soon there was virtually no flexibility in the relationship system of this family.

Diane was less able to resolve the tensions of her family's reactivity than Ivan. Ivan's lack of secrecy about his homosexual lifestyle served to open up relationships in his family in the long run, as well as reduce anxiety in the family's emotional system. He gained self-confidence from his own openness and from his continued meaningful contacts and exchanges with many of his relatives. His behavior helped to create a new family out of the original relatively closed relationship conditions.

By contrast, Diane's secrecy and anxiety about her hidden, forbidden life closed the emotional relationships in her family. All her family members were hurt, and to some extent harmed, by her fear and reluctance to be forthcoming about her intimacy with Mavis.

This outcome in Diane's family is clearly less advantageous than that experienced in Ivan's family. In the long run, family members accepted Ivan as an equal and continued to interact with him and his parents in supportive ways. Ivan's family's flexibility of reactions ensured that new family forms and processes emerged. These are conducive to the growth and maturation of all family members.

BEYOND STATUSES

Families are levelling experiences for us all, in that we cannot escape from their influence on the quality of our lives (Hanscombe & Forster, 1982; Hays & Mindel, 1973; Hill, 1949). Generally speaking, most of us participate emotionally in some kind of family (Gilmour & Duck, 1986; Gelfand & Barresi, 1987). The most significant issue for individual and family well-being is not what statuses we have, but how we function with others in our family emotional systems (Blumstein & Schwartz, 1983). What are the qualities of the bonds in our families? How autonomous are we as we strive to live in accordance with our highest goals?

Our abilities to respond to others do not just happen by virtue of having a particular gender or sexual orientation (Lewis & Sussman, 1986; Pollack & Vaughn, 1987; Stoller, 1990), just as adults are not necessarily mature individuals (Price, 1988; Kreppner & Lerner, 1989; Kingson, Hirshorn, & Cornman, 1986). Children are not inevitably victims of family emotional processes, even though they tend to be dependent on their parents' behavior until they are adults in their own right (Beal & Hochman, 1991; Johnson & Barer, 1987).

One challenge of understanding families is to appreciate their evolutionary origins, while deliberately moving into the next stage of development. Our families make us different from each other, as none of us necessarily conforms to statistical norms or trends (Becker, 1963). We can say yes or no to the broad social influences in our lives. We do this more effectively when we come to terms with the emotional processes of our own families (Klein & Aldous, 1988; Koos, 1973). New families emerge when individuals refuse to be pawns in the emotional processes of their families and of wider society.

Chapter 11

Have Fun with Family Bonds!

Although the nature of our family bonds may sometimes have serious, even deadly, consequences for all family members (Aldous & Hill, 1965), we can also be playful and lighthearted as we keep our family relationships viable and fulfill our needs and interests, as well as those of our relatives (Farrell, 1974; Dunn, 1985). We need humor in our lives. Even when our families are in a severe crisis–such as immediately before, during, or after a relative's death–there are appropriate ways to dilute the emotional intensity that predictably engulfs family members at these times.

To become more objective about ourselves and our families, we must first see who we are and recognize our potential for being and doing (Zurcher, 1983; Dahrendorf, 1959). Once we have accomplished this, we can begin to create and sustain healthier family bonds (Fein, 1988; Hanson & Bozett, 1985). As we invent ways to discover ourselves and our capabilities, we come to realize that these important and serious tasks can also be enjoyable leisure pursuits (Haley, 1976).

INNOVATIVE BONDING

A few innovative ways to strengthen family bonds are suggested below. Any of these approaches–or combinations of strategies described–can make contacts with relatives more meaningful than routine or ritual usually allows. Continued efforts to accomplish these activities are necessary, however, as only fairly frequent exchanges with family members can be a basis for the formation and perpetuation of healthy bonds (Hanscombe & Forster, 1982; Laing, 1971; Fischer, 1986).

Family Tree

One way to distill abundant information about a family's history is to diagram collected facts as a family tree. A family tree need not be drawn to scale accurately or systematically, although it should include as long a period of time and as many relatives as possible in its representations.

Dates of births, marriages, deaths, and migrations; reasons for deaths; facts about occupations, geographical locations, and other special characteristics of relatives are useful pieces of information to include. When this drawing of a family tree is complete, it is creative and constructive to circulate it to other family members for their attention and interest. This communication is also an effective tool for gathering further information about any given family.

Perhaps the days have gone when family trees are embroidered as samplers or painted as pictures to be mounted and displayed in living rooms. You may prefer modern day variants to finalize your family history, such as computer graphics or statistical tables. Any shorthand method that summarizes your family history information will help present an overview of your research accurately. It will also be an effective means of disseminating your family tree knowledge to relatives, especially to isolated ones who know relatively little about your family.

Locating Lost Relatives

Any family history or family tree reveals gaps in information about present and past family members. Trying to make contact with relatives–most especially with relatives who may have been spurned by the rest of the family–about detailed information that is lacking is a valuable activity. Eventually these efforts will effectively bridge cut-offs in family communications, and at the same time activate a broader emotional system base for that family.

Initial contacts with lost relatives may be best accomplished through well-timed telephone calls or letters. "Outsider" relatives are frequently responsive and grateful to be contacted, particularly on anniversaries of loved one's deaths, or other sentimental occasions, including special holidays such as Christmas or New Year. A follow-up visit, in person, is the most effective way to make sure that your initial contact turns out to be as positive and as meaningful as possible for all concerned.

Letters

Letters are an unambiguously reliable and responsible means of forming bonds with relatives. They allow us to carefully think through what we want to say, and to succinctly verbalize our deepest concerns. Although culturally speaking we may have lost much of our former interest in the art of letter writing, this is still an effective means that can be depended on for making meaningful contact with relatives.

When we write personal letters, rather than mass-produced chain letters, we are more able to readily establish a sincere tone in our inquiries or requests for information. If the subjects we want to raise with our relatives are sensitive, however, it may be more considerate and more fruitful to make this kind of discreet communication during a personal visit rather than through a letter. It is easier to deal with the consequences of emotionally charged communications responsibly when we are present rather than absent.

The timing for sending letters selectively to our relatives is crucial. It is advisable to acknowledge the most important events in our families through some kind of correspondence if we cannot be present at these special occasions, although sending flowers with a note can be an effective substitute for writing a letter. Relatives are frequently more open to family contacts during crises or celebrations than at other times.

Sometimes writing angry letters, which you have no intention of sending, is an effective way to dilute strong negative feelings such as resentments and anger which have built up from the past. This is a dramatic way to verbalize deepest sentiments without heedlessly destroying the feelings or well-being of the family members in question.

Writing letters to deceased family members can also help to resolve residual grief and anger. The act of writing about your deepest feelings, particularly as you address these directly to your loved or hated ones, is predictably therapeutic since it reduces anxieties and concerns.

Photographs–Old and New

Photographs are objective records of family membership and participation. Much interesting information is captured and distilled through the act of taking and collecting photographs, including contributions from different relatives. Photograph exchanges and viewings are valuable, meaningful means of family communication, as well as sources for interesting continuing conversations.

Photographs can be copied and circulated in a variety of ways. The problem of identifying family members in old photographs can be profitably shared among many family members rather than be a frustrating individual task.

Old family photographs are frequently stored in hidden places and may not be unearthed until relatives die. Whenever we sort relatives' belongings after death, or have contact with others when they are doing this, we need to pay close attention to the variety of photographs that will inevitably surface. Someone in your family will most probably value these photographs, even if they do not mean much to you. Or, you can hold on to them for later viewings or for posterity.

Poetry for Special Occasions

Poetry can express deep feelings, and can be used to commemorate family events in emotionally significant ways. Poems can mark special occasions or say something humorous to and about your family.

One advantage of poetry is that it can either be spoken aloud or read silently. Poems spoken at weddings or funerals can communicate meanings beyond our typically more banal commentaries or conversations. Poems circulated in letters reach a wider audience. At the same time they can summarize our innermost thoughts and feelings meaningfully and gracefully.

Children may be particularly skilled at writing poetry, and frequently elderly family members also enjoy writing poems as a hobby. These creative forms of communication civilize and facilitate our abilities to say things to each other that might otherwise be difficult to verbalize.

Pictures

Other art forms that can be used for meaningful communication among family members are drawing and painting pictures. Pictures may be even more useful as a shorthand method of communication than poetry, in that pictures have messages that go beyond words. One of the most effective ways to disseminate pictures is to send them to family members at festive seasons of the year, such as holiday times, or at times of loss and celebration.

Drawing or painting pictures is an especially useful way for children to communicate their feelings and ideas to adults. When there has been a severe family trauma such as the loss of a parent or incest, a child's pictures may be an essential tool for discovering family problems, and a way for the child to express strong fears and other intense negative feelings. Relationships can be built, and trust developed, by encouraging continued emotionally difficult communications through drawing pictures.

Vacations

If family members resist our efforts to make contact with them, especially when we suggest visiting them, we can plan vacations to take us geographically close to where our relatives live. Visiting them in this way will mean that they will not be the central purpose of our travel. Yet we may be able to make meaningful contacts through casual, spontaneous visits. Relatives are frequently glad to see us when we are far from home, and keeping in touch with them through our travels is an interesting and effective way to bond.

Visiting or inviting geographically distant family members to celebrate major events, like a marriage, is a traditional means of keeping in touch. In the past, attendance at these events may have been motivated more by a sense of obligation than real concern or curiosity. Today, however, family visits can take on a new kind of meaning and mission. This will happen most especially in new families. Family visits are adventures in self-knowledge and invaluable guides on our quests to discover our family origins.

Vacation or weekend travel can be used to attend occasions where many family members are congregated. We learn a great deal about ourselves from seeing how our families interact, and we are able to update our family histories by requesting current information about our less-known relatives. Chances are that family members will volunteer news items since, by this time, we will have established our interest in knowing what is going on.

Tours

Another way to make contact with relatives is to plan a trip expressly to visit several relatives who live out of town. If we combine visits to different family members, we can create a tour. This plan enables us to let each part of the family know what the rest is doing as we move from home to home and town to town. Even though our relatives may not readily show that they are interested in one another, they are usually more than receptive to this kind of information, finding exchanges of information about their families irresistible.

Newsletters

A more formal way to keep in touch with relatives, and one which may not be well received because it is more impersonal than some of the other means discussed, is to circulate a periodic newsletter among relatives. Even though a newsletter may appear to be somewhat mechanistic, especially if we have our letters printed or copied, it is a valuable means of contact when we have large families and are very busy. It is clearly advantageous to send a newsletter when our choice is between sending one or not sending anything.

Be ready to surface from the criticism you will get from pursuing this venture. Know that regular contact with many family members helps build a viable new family and keeps that family's communication system open. This effort has invaluable consequences for all relatives. Furthermore, having the reputation as a writer of a family newsletter enables us to gather additional information more easily as time goes by.

Even though we may not choose to be known as the relative who is always ready to receive information, there are benefits to performing this function. Those family members who are best-informed about their families are more aware of the quality and nature of family emotional processes. They act in their own self-interest more easily than those who know less and are consequently less aware of patterns in their family interactions. Members of new families are sufficiently knowledgeable about their family systems that they are unlikely to fall victim to their potentially destructive characteristics.

Telephone Calls–Near and Far

Telephone calls with family members are sometimes difficult to manage. Our calls may be viewed by others as a nuisance, or they may be perceived as a threat to their privacy. Also, long-distance calls, particularly those to other countries, run up costly telephone bills, especially since it is difficult to curtail intimate exchanges with strong emotional content.

All in all, however, telephone calls have a distinct advantage in that they are both personal and casual. When we place a telephone call, the other party knows that we have made a special effort to contact them. Furthermore, they have the freedom to easily end any conversation they do not want to have.

Sometimes relatives are flattered by our attempts to stay in touch by telephone, especially if they live at a distance from us. Even though they may not be sufficiently interested to contact us, they may be consistently pleased to hear from us when we call them. Our only significant dilemma in this situation is to know how much we can do without experiencing burn-out, or without running up emotional and material costs that we may ultimately resent.

Continuing Conversations

Most communications with family members are continuing conversations. Because families are characterized by their continuity through time, maintaining meaningful exchanges on a long-term basis is more possible with our families than with other small groups.

It is important to cultivate a spirit of continuing conversation with family members. Whatever circumstances evolve, contact should remain open. Ruptures in communications are harmful to those directly involved, and they ultimately affect the rest of the family. However many crises we have to cope with, our frame of mind should be one of touching base with relatives, and of keeping in touch with them.

Silence

When we are convinced that everything has been said that needs to be said, and when we find that other family members are passive or even resistant to our overtures, this is the time to be purposefully silent for a while. Our silence does not mean that we intend to cut off communications. Rather it suggests that we are either not ready to make the next move or not sure what the next move should be. We can also have faith in silence as a means of communication in its own right. Silence can demonstrate great trust and confidence as well as have negative connotations.

Silence may also be an especially effective way to communicate our thoughtfulness and consideration of family members when we have already established satisfactory communication with them. It is better to be missed because there is a change of pace in our communications than to not be noticed because we had no contact in the first place.

Celebrations

It is worth our while to try not to miss the most joyous occasions in our families. It is one thing to be counted on to do what is necessary in hard times and yet another to celebrate for the sake of sharing good times. We will receive considerable emotional dividends from just showing up for special events, whether or not we really want to participate.

There are many ways to show our happiness for those who are celebrating a marriage, birth, or anniversary. We can easily send letters, cards, cables, flowers, or gifts if we cannot be there in person, and this establishes our presence in some way. This lets the celebrants know that we are thinking about them, and that we unequivocally wish them well.

Reunions

Helping plan for a family gathering to take place once a year, or every few years, is a worthwhile activity. These occasions renew our bonds with relatives we do not see frequently, and they allow us to collect information about what other family members are doing as time goes by.

Reunions should not be held too regularly or too frequently, since relatives must not feel pressured to attend or tired of making the effort to come together. If possible, the circumstances of these gatherings should be both pleasurable and easy to manage. People generally do not have sufficient energy left from daily chores to be able to expend much more for family reunions at weekends or on holidays.

FAMILY DISCOVERIES

Outcomes of these ventures depend largely on a person's level of desire to bond with their family members. The kinds of discoveries made (through varied contacts with family members) depend on the scope and intensity of the search.

Two examples of relationship changes within families will show some of the many possibilities for growth and empowerment through innovative family bonding. New families maintain the flexible and durable bonds because they nurture support for a wide variety of family exchanges on a long-term basis. The strongest new families stay rooted in their past generations, while maintaining open, egalitarian relationships rather than closed, hierarchical bonds.

Angela did not know much about her father's family, as her father had died when she was five years old. Both she and her older sister considered their family to be composed of only their mother's relatives.

When Angela started to have her own children, she became more pensive about her life and decided to locate some of her father's relatives. She became so invested in her project that she visited several different states solely to make contact with "lost" relatives. She maintained communications with these family members when her visits were over, and she soon felt as though she belonged to their family. Angela's sister depended on Angela for information about these newly discovered relatives, and soon she too felt as though she belonged to a much larger family than she had known.

The continuing give-and-take between Angela and her father's family gave her increased emotional security. She was able to share this enriched heritage with her young children, and at the same time she resolved some of her negative feelings about her father's death through her exchanges with his relatives. Angela's participation in her father's family allowed her to grieve more effectively for her considerable loss. At the same time she was able to get on with her own life in more satisfying ways.

*   *   *

Paul came from a large family that met regularly with extended kin for picnics and special occasions. He had access to much family memorabilia, and he decided to compile a detailed family history. This was a relatively easy task for him to accomplish since several relatives had already mapped out much information about several different branches of his family.

While he was assembling this information, Paul realized that one of his great-aunts had given birth to a son without being married. Because no one knew what had happened to this aunt, Paul thought he would try to locate her and her son. He scrutinized different genealogical records and used the help of a private investigator in his great-aunt's home town to discover her whereabouts.

Before long, Paul found out that his great-aunt had died in hospital with an incurable liver complaint a few years ago. Her son, his mother's cousin, had moved to a distant state, and no further information was forthcoming about him. After advertising several times to try to contact his mother's cousin in this particular geographical area, Paul eventually heard that he was alive and well, and eager to meet Paul and his new family.

Because Paul discovered a new family member, his own functioning position in his family changed. He became more respected and more empowered. Graham, his mother's cousin, built a close friendship with him. Although Graham had not been motivated to uncover his own family origins, he was grateful that Paul had cared enough to pursue him and establish contact.

CREATIVE CONTRIBUTIONS

It is important for us to devise our own interesting ways to create and maintain healthy family bonds (Lee, 1980; Mutran & Reitzes, 1984). The more relatives we contact, the more flexible and life-giving these bonds will be. This is the very essence of creating a new family. The more meaningful the bonds we establish, the more satisfying emotional rewards we will reap from our family connections (Sanders & Trystad, 1989).

We need to move out of our nuclear families into extended, more tribal kinship groupings (Kerr & Bowen, 1988). It is through sustaining these kinds of extensive contacts that we are able to establish our most effective bonds with our families (Hays & Mindel, 1973; Atkinson, Kivett, & Campbell, 1986). The nature of our bonding helps us resolve the past effectively and move more freely into the future (Caplow, 1968; Cohler, 1983). These are the ways in which we establish new families that will cope best with the myriad pressures of everyday life in our modern industrial societies.

Chapter 12

Birth, Marriage, Death

Optimally, families are our primary means of health and well-being, not merely sources of obligation (Mutran & Reitzes, 1984). If we want to live fully and meaningfully, we must try to maintain a viable connectedness to our families rather than retreating from them (Papp, 1983).

Births, marriages, and deaths are usually the most significant transitions in all different kinds of families' emotional systems (Hill, 1949; Goody, 1962). These are critical periods for many reasons, not the least of which is that significant family members are added or lost at these times. Since families have lifetime memberships, we must essentially group and regroup at such turning points.

SETTING THE SCENE

Understanding the main distinctions between the characteristics of open and closed family systems helps us see how births, marriages, and deaths come to have varying consequences for a wide range of families (Bowen, 1978). Although family relationships are neither completely open nor completely closed, these two extreme conditions clearly illustrate some of the many adaptations families use to reestablish equilibrium after inevitable shifts occur through births, marriages, and deaths (Komarovsky, 1962; Klein & Aldous, 1988).

Those families that are relatively open have flexible relationship bonds. In open families, members are added or lost without too many disruptive effects on the whole emotional system. Open families are functional and they adapt effectively–life goes on constructively in these families fairly soon after they have made the necessary adjustments to additions or losses. Even though open families may experience dramatic or deep crises, they are healed relatively quickly and effectively.

In contrast to open families, closed families may never fully recover from stresses that follow in the wake of inevitable additions and losses. The bonds of relatively closed families are so rigid and brittle that they do not allow their members to adapt easily to significant changes around births, marriages, and deaths. When the emotional system equilibrium of a closed family is not effectively reestablished after these major events, acute or chronic stresses predictably continue for long periods of time and may, in fact, never be effectively resolved.

Since life and growth dynamics include a wide range of emotional processes, it is possible to change a family relationship system from a state of relative closure to relative openness, or vice versa. When even only one family member copes effectively with critical turning points like births, marriages, and deaths, that person can gradually open up the family's emotional system. However, when no deliberate effort is made to maintain the openness of a family emotional system, stress and anxiety will inevitably tighten its bonds, and relationships will move toward closure.

BIRTH

Whatever the specific circumstances of a birth, this major event has emotional consequences for its immediate participants, and for the whole family. Whether a child is born within marriage or not is not as emotionally significant for a family as the attitudes of that child's parents and other family members toward the birth. However, since many people tend to have conventional thoughts and expectations, family members' feelings frequently conform to social stereotypes and to what public opinion defines as acceptable or unacceptable standards of behavior (Freud, 1958; Friedman, 1985).

Ideally, each parent should have a more or less equally positive emotional investment in the birthing process, so that they both welcome their child through favorable anticipation of parental responsibilities (Dally, 1982; Eggebeen & Uhlenberg, 1985). Even though such a constructive and supportive orientation is not possible in many circumstances, a clearly shared parental acknowledgement of birth as a major event proves to be a sufficiently adequate preparation for the necessary adaptation of both child and parents.

If parents, as well as other family members, have negative attitudes about a pending birth, that birth will tend to be a more serious crisis for that family. Traumatic events around births–a father abandoning his family, or a mother giving up her child for adoption–have a strong impact on the whole family. This is true even if these actions are kept secret and then sometimes more so (Falicov, 1988). The process of opening up such relatively closed family emotional systems frequently begins with revealing secrets and establishing open communications among all family members.

One of the most constructive contributions family members can make, either men or women, is to help prepare for a birth or care for a new child. Gender traditions are modified more effectively during crises than in everyday routines, and each family member can benefit through giving direct and tangible expressions of interest in a baby.

When parents give birth, they are supported through the presence and useful actions of those emotionally closest to them. No nuclear family is sufficiently stable to bear the trauma of a birth without some kind of external support. Kin groups are useful and necessary supports at these times (Dean et al., 1989; Colleta & Lee, 1983).

First knowledge of a pregnancy is a critical phase in the birth sequence. A new child takes shape in people's minds as well as in a mother's body, and this shift away from usual attitudes is important to acknowledge and manage (Cohler & Grunebaum, 1981; Fischer, 1981).

Protecting the physical well-being of a newborn and mother is not solely a father's responsibility. Ideally, all family members participate in this task to ensure that mother and child are both physically and emotionally comfortable in the first days or weeks after the birth. New fathers also need to be protected. Although transitions in their lives are culturally distinct from those of new mothers, births also create traumatic changes for fathers.

Mother-daughter bonds usually intensify when daughters give birth, especially when a daughter's first child is born. Optimally this closeness does not exclude the active physical and emotional participation of fathers and sons in birthing events. Both women and men need to interact during these significant emotional processes if they are all to have fulfilling lives.

MARRIAGE

Marriages are more social happenings than births, since they generally include more participants and more complex ritual exchanges. Weddings accomplish formal unions of two individuals and two families at one time and in one place, and their celebrations are more overt and more organized than births.

Preliminary stages of marriage vary considerably. These differences go far beyond social class and ethnic distinctions. There are many varieties of families within the same social class or same ethnic group. Do a couple's families know each other? Do they approve of the marriage? Was a couple engaged? Have the partners lived together? How long have they known each other? Variations in these kinds of significant lead-ins to marriage mean that the qualities of wedding festivities and family emotional processes differ markedly both at the time of marriage and during the aftermath.

The emotional dependencies that inevitably surface during the different phases of marriages are significant evidence of the family emotional system. These aspects of weddings need to be considered and evaluated more directly than the usual conventional concerns about ostentatious show. The true feelings of couples must be acknowledged, as well as those of their relatives. At the very least the major participants in a wedding should know and understand the emotional tone of both families.

Families that are not accustomed to assembling in one place will find any wedding stressful merely due to the fact that their members are meeting together for this special occasion. Exchanges before, during, and after wedding ceremonies provide a great deal of information about family emotional systems. Family members, including the bride and groom, will benefit from a deliberate effort to observe and learn about their family dependencies during this event. No family transition is so smooth or so ceremonious that participants can afford to ignore the significance of either overt or underlying patterns of interaction.

DEATH

Deaths are the most critical emotional family events that can occur, giving the most stress to the largest proportion of their family members (Durkheim, 1951; Anderson, 1984). Although it makes a considerable difference whether a particular death is an acute short-term event or a chronic long-term process (McNeely & Colen, 1983), in the final analysis all deaths are severe, permanent losses to the family emotional system.

If deceased family members have held leadership positions in their families, they are missed more than those who have not played such significant roles. Accordingly, the loss of a young family member frequently does not have as great an impact on a family's emotional system as does the loss of an active older person.

A death frequently precipitates a major shift between members of different generations and determines a personal loss. In the normal course of affairs, as a generation of grandparents dies off in a particular family, a generation of parents becomes grandparents. This means that once more some of the lifetime continuities of family membership are brought vividly and dramatically into play through family losses and replacements.

Being present for deaths and funerals is an effective way for us to come to terms with our own deaths, and with the deepest feelings stirred up in our families. Ideally, gender roles should not dictate how we express our grief or caring. It is not women's unambiguous responsibility to look after sick family members, or to tend to family concerns at times around a death. Blood ties are more significant than convention. Those who are most directly related to a dying person need to participate directly in that death in order to be able to let go of their attachment to the deceased relative and get on with their lives.

Death is a severe emotional transition, as well as a time of serious financial adjustment or dislocation, and every family member participates in this emotional loss in some way. Knowing the extent of a particular loss, and what a loss really means, can make for liberating rather than oppressive experiences.

GROWTH

Inescapable as birth, marriage, and death are, it is not accurate to think that we necessarily grow from their occurrence. If we retreat or deny the importance of these major emotional events, our rejection of significant opportunities to participate in our most intense family processes delays or retards our adaptation to them, as well as our ongoing maturation. We need to go directly into the vortex of changes in our families at such critical times if we want to truly mold our lives.

If we are able to grow during the occurrence of birth, marriage, and death in our families, the kind of maturation that ensues is more hardy and more enduring than other kinds of personal development. Even though we may consider it in our interest to earn academic credentials or acquire social skills, these achievements pale beside the advantages we gain from the emotional growth we automatically attain through participation in our families' exchanges during crises. Furthermore, benefits from our active involvement in family crises affect us at much deeper levels of being, and for longer periods of time, than intellectual or conventional learning.

AFTERMATH

Sometimes it may not be the actual events of birth, marriage, and death themselves that instigate our growth, but rather the aftermath of these changes. We must be aware of the emotional significance of seemingly unrelated consequences of birth, marriage, and death in our families in order to benefit fully from these shifts in the regular patterns of interaction.

It usually takes at least one year for the family emotional systems to reestablish equilibrium after birth, marriage, or death, and it is also particularly during this extended period of time that new opportunities to grow and mature will arise for all family members. A constructive attitude to have during the aftermath of these events is to be ready and willing to participate in family activities when needed. We must not allow ourselves to become subservient to other family members, or to be exploited. Rather we must make our presence felt through contributing something constructive to our relatives.

If you are a practical person who enjoys being directly helpful or useful to others, participating in your family activities when needed during these aftermaths may mean no more than consistently giving to others at these times. There need be no grand plan for participation or special motives beyond expressing yourself meaningfully. Also, however, if you merely keep in touch with your relatives, and establish your interest and concern for what is going on in your family at these times, this will benefit you as well as other family members. When morale is low or in jeopardy, your benign presence, support, and experience are valued more highly.

TRANSITIONS

One of the most useful ways to view birth, marriage, and death is to see them as crucial transitions in family life cycles. At these times of rapid change, patterns show how entire family systems undergo transformations. Shifts in one part of a family inevitably affect other parts, especially those parts which are most closely related to the members who were recently born, married, or died.

Two examples show how these transitions permeate different generations in a family. These observations can be made because it frequently takes about a year of dislocation in familiar behavioral patterns until a family can reestablish its equilibrium after one of these major life cycle events.

> Geoffrey looked forward to introducing his fiancée, Jane, to his parents and grandparents. He was surprised to discover, however, that neither his mother nor his grandmother liked Jane. They were both disconcerted about his coming marriage. Geoffrey was not aware that his functional position as an only son and an only grandson would mean that when he pulled a substantial amount of his "regular" attention away from his

family (as a result of his marriage) his behavior would upset many of the usual behavioral patterns in his family.

After his wedding, Geoffrey visited his mother and grandmother frequently with his new wife. As both Geoffrey's mother and grandmother continued to criticize Jane harshly, it did not take long before she did not want to spend time with them any more. This reactive negativity between Jane and Geoffrey's mother and grandmother continued throughout the period when Geoffrey and Jane raised their two small children. It did not change substantially until Geoffrey's grandmother died.

*   *   *

Yvonne had been her father's favorite daughter throughout her life, even though she had two older sisters. She spent many of her weekends visiting her parents after she left home, talking with her father more than her mother as she recounted what was going on in her life.

Yvonne was not aware of the intensity of her attachment to her father until her father died suddenly of a brain tumor. She was distraught to see him suffer, and even more upset when he did not recover from his brief, painful illness.

For a year Yvonne was not able to date, socialize, or enjoy herself. She became accident-prone and fell several times during this period of time. She was unable to visit her mother without blaming her for her father's illness, and she stubbornly refused to see members of her father's family in spite of her intense grief.

Yvonne gradually became more accepting of her loss, as well as more objective about it. As a result she was able to reestablish contact with her mother and some of her relatives in her father's family. She started to visit her father's older brother frequently, perhaps because he strongly resembled her father and because he too suffered greatly from the loss of his brother. As Yvonne became emotionally reconnected with her family, she stopped having accidents and was able to get on with her life effectively once more.

PREPARATIONS

Birth, marriage, and death can essentially prepare us for experiencing some of the advantages of continuities in our family cycles. Our new families are those which are more fully integrated across time and space, and which exhibit tenacious strengths due to expressed continuities in their emotional system.

We grow stronger from what we learn emotionally during major transitions in our families. This strengthening and maturation means that we will be able to contribute to others more adequately when crises recur. Furthermore, when we have learned how to grow through these major events, we will be more likely to grow in the future whenever opportunities present themselves.

Our active participation in family life cycle events means that we automatically prepare ourselves for other aspects of our lives. The superior levels of functioning in new families prepare us for more effective social participation. As social events are generally considerably less demanding and less stressful than birth, marriage, and death, we are more able to deal with our social lives after we have resolved our family crises.

Our worldviews and beliefs about reality necessarily depend, in large part, on our family experiences. If we are members of hostile, life-threatening families, we may have to protect ourselves by withdrawing or limiting our participation in these destructive emotional systems. We must know when and how to leave lethal families, or toxic parts of families, so that we can find or create substitute families from people we can count on for a lifetime.

We each need a meaningful and reliable group in which we can prepare and support ourselves for the exigencies of life and death. When we understand deeply what others' lives and deaths are all about, we are in better positions to live fully and die meaningfully. Birth, marriage, and death teach us valuable lessons; they provide us with our most meaningful opportunities to examine, formulate, and reformulate our most cherished values and our closest dependencies and relationships.

Chapter 13

Making a Will

Our participation in birth, marriage, and death broadens our perspectives and brings us gains in maturity (Bettelheim, 1987). Particularly when we come to terms with significant deaths, we strengthen our capacities for realism through accepting the limits of life in general and our own lives in particular (Hoerning & Schaeffer, 1984).

Our ability to create and live in new families depends on this kind of maturity and perspective. When we order our affairs in anticipation of our deaths, we become involved in not only preparing for what we hope will be the most favorable circumstances possible for our deaths but in creating a plan for the most meaningful distribution of our resources (Cheal, 1983). It is only at death that we almost inevitably show what we have accomplished, and what we most want to give to or take away from others, especially our relatives (Cates & Sussman, 1982).

One of the most significant ways we come to terms with our own lives and deaths is to assume the responsibility for making our wills. In these documents we generally express our deepest values and strongest beliefs through our personal, informed directions for the distribution of our assets. We may also choose to make a living will in which we communicate how we prefer to die if we are not able to make our own decisions about our well-being at that time. In a living will we may wish to clarify whether we want extraordinary medical measures to be taken to prolong our lives, whatever the circumstances are that we find ourselves in that we cannot control.

As well as including the distribution of our assets, we can include detailed statements about our preferences for funeral services, disposal of our bodies, and allocation of our most prized personal possessions. In this way we can also essentially fully orchestrate our last rites, and write our own obituaries. Beyond these particular measures we can use other creative ways to write our wills and let our final wishes be known.

OTHERS' WILLS

One guide for making our own wills is to read wills that deceased members of our families have already drawn up. As well as showing us how and why major decisions were made in our families, those wills stand as tangible evidence of the most important values of our relatives who wrote them.

Patterns of wealth, property, or personal belonging distribution among members of different generations show how repeated forms and processes of dependencies are passed on and carried into the future (Eggebeen & Uhlenberg, 1985; Engels, 1955). Families frequently devise distinctive ways to assemble and divide their assets, according to particular gender preferences or specific affectionate alliances, for example (Goody, 1962). Early deaths may be characterized by unusual bequests, especially when a death is unexpected; deaths in old age generally reflect more serious pondering and incorporate a variety of symbolic gestures made to the youngest family members (Goffman, 1959).

Even though the reasons for looking at the wills of our family members may be purely practical (that is, to see how these wills were constructed), their substance shows us a great deal about the personal preferences of our deceased relatives, and about the broadest patterns of interaction in our families. Wills are significant pieces of knowledge, and hard evidence of what final decisions were made. We must appreciate how the facts revealed in wills go beyond specific information about relatives' material goods. They are direct indicators of the primary values of the deceased members who wrote the wills. And they are accurate reflections of personal likes and dislikes.

Will-reading and will-writing are serious and difficult, yet rewarding, activities. We can discover some of our deepest family values by examining the wills of deceased family members. Even though it may be difficult to locate relatives' wills, it is worth the necessary effort since family members who keep wills–or have access to them–are also likely to know interesting, even critical information, about our families. Will-keepers have special, privileged positions in family emotional systems (Mills, 1959; Lee & Ellithorpe, 1982).

DECIDING TO BE OUT OF STEP

When we have considered all the possibilities for making our own wills, we must decide if we are going to do what we think is expected of us or be idiosyncratic in our disbursements of assets. At this apparent final reckoning of our values, we are forced into deciding who and what is really important to us.

Even though we are not able to concern ourselves about what others think of us after death, our wills are essentially one of our most important statements of what we want others to remember about us (Toman, 1976; Sussman & Burchinal, 1962). If we decide to go too far beyond custom when choosing ways to distribute our assets, our closest relatives may have to live with the consequences of our choices with inconvenience and difficulty. Making our wills is not a trivial act with short-range consequences. Before we go out on a limb to specify unusual bequests and requests, we should consider what our relatives might need from us as they try to grow and live fully after we have died.

DOING THINGS OUR WAY

Writing our wills is not usually our last living act. Rather the content and intentions of our wills are specific, dramatic ways to make our presence felt immediately after our deaths. Our wills are our final words to the world and to our families. These are our last efforts and last available means to express our values through direct communication with our families.

Making our wills provides us with opportunities to do things our own way. If we do not make our wills, the legal system or other family members will have their say in ways that we might not choose. It is because the acts involved in making our wills are so profoundly personal, with far-reaching consequences, that these tasks and privileges should not be missed.

Whether we decide to be conventional or idiosyncratic when distributing our resources, lawyers are able to advise us about our options. This resource allows us to make specific decisions in order to accomplish our preferred objectives. Unless we establish our priorities clearly, we may easily miss the essence of what we really want to do, especially when others advise and instruct us on every aspect of the logistics of making a will. It is not easy to create the wills we want, but drawing up a will can be a means of substantial emotional growth and fulfillment, and a way to strengthen our new families.

MAKING OUR WILLS KNOWN

Once we have completed our wills, it is useful, and enlightening, to discuss relevant parts of them with those who will be most affected by our deaths. Talking about the administrative and substantive details surrounding our own future deaths can be unequivocally meaningful and practical rather than morbid.

These exchanges are made most effectively when we deliberately select pleasant settings or special occasions like birthdays or anniversaries. It is not easy to concentrate on such an emotional topic as the likely circumstances of our deaths, and we need supportive and congenial settings for such personal communication.

The act of giving loved ones information about our final wishes is a bonding experience that will be remembered, by us and the others involved. If we deny our deaths, and irresponsibly opt to avoid making wills, we will forever try to attain this kind of intimacy in our relationships unsuccessfully. Accomplishing the difficult task of compiling our wills to our own satisfaction launches us into new levels or stages of living.

When we tell our relatives what our final wishes are, we become free of some of our past responsibilities to them and to ourselves. This lessening of our moral burdens gives us more freedom in the years to follow. Making our wills known publicizes our innermost wishes to some extent, thus making those wishes more real to us.

This phase of personal growth strengthens our identities and integrates self, thereby improving the flexibility of our bonds in our new families.

FREEDOMS EXPERIENCED THROUGH MAKING OUR WILLS

Making our wills evokes our deepest levels of self and our most personal experiences. These tasks require us to face our lives and our deaths simultaneously. The more isolated we are from our families in our daily lives–the more we retreat from reality–the more we will eventually need to make our wills. Our lives come full circle, and we discover how to live completely, only when we see our deaths in the context of our families as we continue to live.

When assessing the ways we want to distribute our resources, we must make decisions about who and what are important to us. For many people, those who are most important to them are also those who are emotionally closest. Our children and grandchildren, or our brothers and sisters, frequently become our main beneficiaries. A review of the contents of many wills shows that families are consistently the most emotionally significant groups to which we belong (Lamb, 1987). For this reason it is relatively rare to go beyond family circles when distributing worldly goods at the time of death.

When we complete our wills, we frequently find we have resolved some of our most persistent relationship concerns with the family members who are closest to us–or with those who will receive most of our assets when we die. The act of writing our wills frees us from some of the restrictiveness of our most binding emotional ties. We become more able to get on with our lives than we were before we wrote our wills.

WILLS AT ANY AGE

Even though it is older people rather than younger who tend to make their wills, the young can also benefit a great deal from making their wills. In some respects, the younger we are when we make our wills, the freer we are to live fully from that time forward. The longer phase of emotional freedom that younger people experience by making their wills becomes a real bonus from the perspective of the life course.

Making a will means that we take responsibility for our deaths as well as our lives, even though our actions do not necessarily mean that we have multiple assets to distribute (Rubin, 1976). If we are to live fully, the emotional advantages of making our wills must be respected and valued more than calculations of dollar amounts.

Reflection helps us make sense of our lives and come to terms with both our desires and our disappointments. The perspective we are forced to take when contemplating the specifics of our own deaths is necessarily one of the broadest views we can get of our lives. This breadth of vision gives us special opportunities to assess how we want to live now, and how we want to spend the rest of our lives.

Just as our families generate their own emotional processes, so do our own views of ourselves. For example, our self-perceptions largely determine our desired goals and contributions to others. By acknowledging what we want to accomplish before the end of our lives, we become freer to invest ourselves in present actions. In this way, making our wills empowers us to move more freely into our futures with enthusiasm as well as meaning. Even though we may have relatively few years left to live after making our wills, this time will be spent in more rewarding and enriching ways than would have been possible if our wills had not been written. Making our wills is life-affirming as well as freeing.

PRACTICAL RESULTS

The following two examples provide contrasting views of some specific advantages of making wills. Fred made his will in his mid-thirties; Fiona made her will after her husband died, when she was over 60 years old.

The circumstances of both Fred and Fiona show how the longest-lasting and most powerful positive consequences of making wills affect functional positions in family emotional systems. Making their wills strengthened their positions in relation to their family members and friends. It also added security and connectedness with their past, present, and future.

Even though Fred was a relatively young man of 34, having a wife and two small children prompted him to assume the responsibility of making a family will. As the younger son of his original family, he had been extremely close to his parents and had not needed to be accountable for his actions. Although he had delayed marrying for some time, he now found that his situation had changed dramatically.

When Fred began to assess his final wishes about resources and possessions, he necessarily became more emotionally detached from his parents and, at the same time, more focused on his own family. This process enabled him to see his position in his family more clearly, and he subsequently placed more value on his relationship with his wife and children. The will-making experience provided him with a new base for family interaction, and it implied different ways of interacting with his significant others. The decisions he made in order to compose his will gave him a more realistic and more vital sense of who he was and could be.

*   *   *

Fiona was widowed when she was 60 years old. She was very shocked by the sudden death of her husband and reactively withdrew from her family and friends during the grieving period immediately following her husband's death.

With some prompting from a close woman friend, Fiona became convinced that she needed to make her own will to take care of her affairs and the needs of her two grown children and grandchildren. She had not made an independent will before; she had been satisfied to act as an appendage to her husband–in will-making and most other activities. Therefore, the decisive act of making her own will now, by contrast, made her increasingly aware of herself and her real wishes and desires.

After making her will, Fiona experienced increased peace of mind and a sense of coming to terms with the loss of her husband. Subsequently, she became interested in visiting her family and friends, and no longer withdrew from opportunities to socialize.

Fiona also began to take her grandparenting more seriously and to spend longer periods with her grandchildren. Making her will gave her a sense of having prepared for the future as well as she could, and of being fully responsible in her own right. Since this will-making activity was more autonomous than decisions she had made earlier in her life, she benefited by gaining new strength and influence within her family and social relationships.

Chapter 14

Find the Joy!

To be able and willing to choose the best that life has to offer–individually and collectively–is a sign of our health rather than our depravity (Zurcher, 1983). We have a right and responsibility to be happy, and most of us want to experience joy. Since it is not always easy to know how or where to find joy, its pursuit becomes a goal or a task we set for ourselves, an action we decide to take (Cohler, 1983).

One choice that ultimately offers us increased joy is that of creating a new family. When we choose to have a new family, we move toward having a family that works for us rather than one which robs us of energy and vitality (Farrell, 1974). As members of new families, we can take constructive action in difficult situations rather than be self-destructive or impinge on others' well-being (Goode, 1956). Our new families help us see the good that surrounds us rather than the bad, even though we are aware that the bad exists (Caplan, 1989).

Modern-day pressures on family life frequently make it difficult to find joy in our personal relationships (Bagarozzi & Anderson, 1989). In today's society it is usually easier for us to give up some of our personal investments in intimate relationships and families than to persistently return to them with hopes of finding ourselves there, or of thereby meeting our emotional needs (Beutler et al., 1989). The joy we crave does not come to us easily. The slow warm glow from this kind of fulfillment generally comes only after we experience much frustration and anguish through confronting our weaknesses during exchanges with significant others.

Transcendence–an ecstasy of joy and happiness that lifts us, at least momentarily, above harsh everyday realities–is necessarily hard-won. As we formulate and work toward our own transcendent goals, however, we create realistic survival strategies for ourselves. It is only those goals with a transcendent quality that have the power to carry us beyond the inevitable sadness, grief, and losses we experience through interaction and commitment to families and intimate relationships. Goals that transcend the mundane details of our daily family lives move us predictably and dependably further toward joy.

MAKE THE CHALLENGE

In order to take up the challenge of finding joy in our families, we first have to make this challenge appeal to us by believing that it will actually meet our needs. If we do not believe that our families can indeed satisfy our emotional needs, we will not be able to wholeheartedly take up the challenge to strengthen our bonds with our families (Sussman & Steinmetz, 1987).

When we look at ourselves and society as objectively as possible, we find that most people, whatever their age, are supported by families or significant others in some way (Kivett, 1985; Hoerning & Schaeffer, 1984). To see our families for what they really are and to create new families, however, we must acknowledge that our family connections go deeper and further afield than the parent-child fragments we are accustomed to thinking of as families. If we wish to ultimately find our joy, we need to become aware of the extent and complexity of our intergenerational bonds, and of the extensiveness of the ties we necessarily have with our local communities and social histories.

When we realize that we are links in a long chain of being–mere parts of a whole–we will see both ourselves and that whole more clearly (Swan, 1984; Laing, 1971; Kluckhohn & Strodtbeck, 1961). We accurately understand who we are only when we put ourselves within a broad context (Glassner & Freedman, 1979; Fein, 1988). However, due to the relatively limited scope of our intergenerational relations, it is easier to define who we are in relation to the past generations of our families than in relation to the endless complexities of society at large (Hurvitz, 1979). Our functional position in our families gives us a meaningful context for self-understanding, a viable whole through which we can see and know ourselves (Haley, 1976).

TAKE THE CHALLENGE

Only after we realize how emotionally significant our families are to us can we relate to them in rewarding ways (Dunn, 1985; Fischer, 1986). As we cut through traditional or romantic myths about our families, we begin to wake up more to both the benefits and liabilities of our family connections (Dally, 1982). For just as families can enhance our supreme fulfillment, they also have the potential to be life-threatening and lethal in their effects (Mann, 1988). We need to know what our families are, how to protect ourselves from them, and how to grow by interacting with them constructively (Furstenberg & Spanier, 1984).

The challenge to move more deeply into the realities of our families, thereby leaving romanticized family myths behind us, inevitably threatens some of our most cherished values. However, as high divorce rates in the United States have been strongly influenced by our cultural beliefs in romantic love, moving toward extended kin can give us more realistic and satisfying emotional security. If we expect too much from our personal relationships, we are more likely to give up on them prematurely. When we get reconnected with our kinship ties rather than continue to live fragmented lives, we will be able to discover the profound joy we crave (Hanson & Bozett, 1985).

Taking the challenge to move deeply into both our past and present family dependencies brings us face to face with ourselves more quickly and more effectively than is possible through other kinds of group experiences. We discover who we really are, as well as what we really want to do, when we cut through our families' romances and myths to our more crude but true individual and family strengths.

CHOICES

As we choose to take the challenge to find joy through our families, we become more in charge of our lives. It is only when we know and interact with our families–in both front stage and back stage terms–that we can truly choose ourselves and create new families. We are strongly influenced by our everyday interactions with our families in that our resulting perceptions and beliefs largely dictate how we act, and we ourselves are results of our own actions.

All our choices are significant, as we must decide what we want to do with our time and energy each minute of each hour. Whether or not we are aware of making these choices, we continuously select which values are most important to us, which options we consider, and which goals we pursue. Only when we are autonomous, when we know that it is we who decide what we believe in and what we do, are we capable of finding joy.

We understand ourselves more fully through our families when we choose to identify and clarify our own beliefs–as distinct from those of other family members–about reality. During this process we must be able to know when to say no effectively to our loved ones, as well as when to say yes. Furthermore, we must opt for solitude and for our own counsel, as well as for the companionship and guidance of those closest to us. Although our new families are interdependent, they allow family members to be flexibly autonomous rather than tightly interrelated. Essentially, we honor our uniqueness throughout the painstaking establishment of our new families.

RESPONSIBILITY

Our truest responsibility to ourselves and to others is to live fully. In order to accomplish this, we must know how to meet our emotional needs, create our own delights, and pursue our own goals. Our new families embrace and nurture the attainment of these accomplishments, which in turn serve to develop human potential.

Before we are able to approach ideals of this kind, we have to cope with our demands in the here and now, and realistically assess ourselves. As we inevitably experience dashed hopes and losses, our responsibility is to transcend our sadness through constructive action, not wallow in negative feelings about our disappointments.

When we see where it is that we are going, we will live through our present frustrations more easily. Our progress is impeded by either dwelling in the past or by defining the present as our only reality. Even though it is generally beneficial to know where we are coming from, it is more challenging as well as more interesting to know where we are going–that is, where we are really going, and not where we think we would like to go.

ENJOY LIFE

Ideally, we must find challenges or positions for ourselves that make it possible for us to assume our real responsibilities to enjoy life and be happy. We live fully only when we find joy in our own conscious and deliberate efforts to interact with others. This mature achievement is neither an accident nor a consequence of luck. We must choose to be happy in whatever the circumstances are that we find ourselves in. At the same time we must choose to work toward accomplishing goals that will bring us joy.

When we find that we are not interested in choosing a full life, or cannot choose to enjoy life, we need to reflect about our values as we make other choices. We may even go so far as to choose to remove ourselves from particular situations we find ourselves in, although this is not necessarily our best option. Any choice to enjoy life presents omnipresent challenges, and it is our responsibility to make this awesome choice; no one else can make it for us.

Two examples of how people actually decide to find joy in their lives are outlined below. In the situations that follow, both David and Nancy were able to make changes which increased their life satisfaction.

David began to enjoy his life more once he had defined a clear purpose for himself in his day-to-day behavior. He achieved this by first refusing to follow in his father's foot-steps as a factory worker, an occupation that his parents had pressured him to follow. He then decided to start his own landscaping business in a nearby suburb.

Although the outcome meant that David did not at first earn as much money as would have been possible at a factory, he gained independence and meaning by choosing to do only what he loved most of all. Regardless of the income differential, David continues to have more freedom through running his own landscaping business than he could have possibly achieved in a factory setting. The result of these work choices is that he simultaneously increases his autonomy in relation to his parents and sister.

*   *   *

Nancy began to enjoy her life more after she decided to remain single for the present time. Her family had pressured her greatly to marry, since her parents and brothers did not want her to become dependent on them. Nancy found it difficult, but well worth her while, to pursue her own objectives to remain single in light of these pressures.

Nancy increases her autonomy as she persists in her decision not to follow the emotional, self-serving dictates of her relatives. Her newfound freedom enables her to pursue her long-range career interests for the first time in her life, and as she purposefully accelerates her independent activities, she reduces her everyday stresses.

JOY AND YOUR FAMILY

Our belief in the possibility of experiencing joy is strongly influenced by the nature of our family bonds. New families are open emotional systems with flexible bonds. When we create new families, we are predictably more likely to experience joy. If our family bonds are tight, rigid, and restrictive (characteristic of most traditional and nuclear families), we find ourselves in relatively closed emotional systems, which are less conducive to our discovery of joy.

All too often we react in an overly negative or overly positive fashion to our families. It is unusually difficult to be honest or objective with ourselves when assessing the importance our families have in relation to our happiness. All too frequently we find that we would prefer to move away from our relatives than to engage directly with them through presence and actions.

Historically, goals of independence have usually translated themselves into actions whereby younger members leave their parents to become fully adult. As a result of this cultural trend, it is not always easy for us to understand why premature moves away from our families cannot make us achieve independence or necessarily allow us to become more mature. We only gain independence when we interact with our families on our own terms while maintaining considerable respect for them.

New families increase the possibility that their individual members will experience joy through strengthening members' emotional well-being. We automatically increase the possibility of experiencing joy in our lives when we renew our families through learning to depend on our relatives differently. In order to open up our families, we can no longer continue to do what others tell us. Rather, we must relate responsibly to our families on our terms. This does not mean that we should not be tolerant or considerate of our relatives, nor should we necessarily deliberately confront them. Our responsibility is best achieved by forging our destinies through and in the midst of our daily exchanges with our families. In sum, joy is more attainable when we are rooted in new families, and when we keep our new families open and flexible by nurturing mutually autonomous relationships.

Joy occurs when we live fully and directly in relation to our families, rather than in isolation from them. We cannot deny our innate family dependencies and at the same time be truly independent. If we try to do this, our dependencies will haunt us for as long as we deny them. Our dependencies will inevitably overwhelm us in a variety of ways and through different guises if we do not come to terms with them within the context of our families.

We take up the challenge to find joy when we choose to stay in meaningful touch with our relatives. However, we must make some contact with family members far beyond our spouses and children in order to more effectively claim our true heritages of emotional connectedness to members of past generations. Also, we must deliberately take the support of our family members if they are reluctant to offer it to us readily. We all have an emotional entitlement to family support, even though we may have to go through some of the fires of family passions–anger as well as love–in order to really live what we have chosen for ourselves. These pathways make up our journeys to joy.

Chapter 15

To Be Continued . . .

Life is continuity; and families participate in and symbolize this same continuity (Aries, 1962). Our contacts with others are necessarily unfinished, since we continuously participate in the processes of becoming (Keniston, 1965). It is impossible for us to know reality and human nature definitively because life goes on and we are all constantly moving forward (Mead, 1970).

Circumstances of continuous change in the universe forge our needs for secure bases from which to move into the world (Pfeifer & Sussman, 1991). Families usually perform this security function for us more effectively than other social groups due to their lifetime membership bonds (Saxton, 1990). These facts about our emotional needs do not imply that there is or should be any specific moral virtue attached to maintaining contact with our families, but rather that our families are our most effective means of survival and fulfillment in the long run (Young & Wilmott, 1973).

Throughout our lives we have dreams of creating and sustaining our own families, and of being more successful at loving and rearing our children than our parents were before us (Rubin, 1976). These are worthwhile desires, but we must come to terms with the reality of what love means on a daily basis and how we can best love others without ignoring our own needs or impairing ourselves (Sussman & Steinmetz, 1987).

It is largely in the midst of the emotional reciprocity of our families that we find our true selves (Skolnick & Skolnick, 1989). All other beliefs about our families are essentially little more than idealism, ideology, or philosophy (Slater, 1991). If we do not acknowledge our families as our most effective and most meaningful bases of emotional security, we will inevitably set out on a continuous search for substitutes (Sampson, 1988). As long as we choose to move away from our families, instead of advancing into their connectedness, we will find that we perpetually hide from ourselves rather than grow and mature (Zurcher, 1983).

We nurture ourselves when we make meaningful contact with relatives in the furthest reaches of our families (Strauss, 1978). When we give our attention to the nature of our bonding with the whole family system, rather than merely one or two inner family members, we discover more of ourselves. In fact, we essentially create ourselves through interacting with a sufficient number of significant others (Cohler & Grunebaum, 1981; Cohler, 1983). In this way we live ourselves into being and action rather than dreaming ourselves into unreality (Cooley, 1964; Dahrendorf, 1959). These interpersonal activities create the new families that can fortify and support us (Cancian, 1987).

VALUE OF OUR FAMILIES

We are conditioned to value our families for the sake of an abstract principle of love, instead of being persuaded that it is families' functions of survival and support that ultimately make up their true value for us (Darwin, 1964). Our emotional well-being and capabilities depend largely on the quality of our family relationships, and unless we value our families for what they really are we can destroy ourselves (Dinnerstein, 1977).

Our families are essentially our home bases for the most effective orientations and preparations for living in the world. We must make conscious and deliberate efforts to negate the influences of our families if we want to avoid reflecting our families directly in all our behavior. This basic self-knowledge about the power of our families is an essential first stage in our quest to discover who we are and what we want to do with our lives. Moreover, our family connections will continue to extend to our deepest past, and thereby have a strong impact on our lives, whether we acknowledge this influence or not. Theoretically, we all have an infinite number of ancestors since we are necessarily related to and descended from many different kinds of people.

In order to take the steps necessary to strengthen ourselves through exchanges with our relatives, we may have to make a deliberate effort to value our families more than we do at present. Merely realizing and coming to terms with the pervasiveness of families–in social exchanges, theater, media, popular culture, novels, public affairs–is useful for increasing our awareness and valuing of our own families (Freud, 1958). Recognizing the roles played by families in less developed countries, or in earlier historical periods, is another guide to understanding the continuing personal and global importance of families, whether or not we like this fact (Frazier, 1939).

Entering into this kind of study and reflection about families does not mean that we should accept any particular family form as superior to others (Fischer, 1981; Engels, 1955). In fact, selective preferences for family forms can easily be detrimental to our growth and development, especially since it is family processes rather than family forms that are critical for our well-being. In order to fully understand the nature of family processes, we must cultivate an appreciation for the existing variety of families, as well as the infinite number of possible family forms, rather than tenaciously clinging to particular family types. The sooner we let go of our preconceived ideas about what families should be, the more lifegiving and life-supporting both we and our families can be (Dally, 1982).

VALUES AND OUR FAMILIES

Families tend to present their ideas and views of the world to their children as reality or truth (Farber, 1973). When we observe families in the context of whole societies, we find that they selectively mediate broad social values and transmit only what they value most to their children (Fischer, 1986). As a result of this selectivity, most families reflect social values in partial, often distorted ways rather than transmitting a representative cross-section of social values to their children (Elder & Clipp, 1988). For example, families are significant cultural units of different social classes and ethnic groups, and their strongest values usually result from their affiliation with particular social classes or ethnic groups (Billingsley, 1968).

In these respects, our family worlds are necessarily only integral parts of our larger reality. A significant catalyst of personal growth, which is nurtured by new families, is to become sufficiently free to challenge our families' values and worldviews. In order to accomplish this, we need our own set of values which may or may not be consistent with our families' values (de Beauvoir, 1974).

Our families will predictably resist our autonomy as a consequence of our necessary value differences from other family members (Falicov, 1988). If we do not share all or most of our families' values, we are perceived as a threat to family stability (Goode, 1956). However, when we are able to recognize the intrinsic fluidity of our family structures, in that values are continuously traded within and among families, we can more fully recognize and appreciate the significance of our own value differences. As we begin to express these differences directly to our families, our lives, as well as our families, are renewed.

New families tolerate a much wider range of values among their members than traditional or nuclear families (Hill, 1949). In contrast to this characteristic flexibility of new families, traditional families, and even nuclear families, frequently adhere rigidly to their hierarchical authority structures (Hill et al., 1970). Because traditional and nuclear families are not working effectively in modern societies, or in individual lives, we must find ways to modify their family values constructively. Richer, more viable worldviews need to be transmitted to children–the next generation of adults–rather than the repetition of anachronistic values (Lee, 1980). We are not, and cannot afford to try to be, clones of our parents. We are uniquely and distinctively who we are, in spite of having some family resemblances and imitations (Lynn, 1974).

It is our responsibility to select the values we want to absorb from our families and to apply these deliberately selected values creatively rather than destructively in our daily lives. Our families' values are essentially starting points for discovering our own values. We must interact with these familiar values, as well as participate in social settings outside our families, if we are to develop our true strengths and potential (Mannheim, 1952).

FAREWELLS

By acknowledging our intergenerational connectedness, we grow in mature relationship to our ancestors and pass the torch to younger family members in inspiring ways (Goody, 1962). When we tell young relatives what our lives have been and are, and what we believe in, we give them an invaluable broader perspective on their own lives (Lamb, 1987). We must let go of our individual and social illusions if we are to grow and live fully (Johnson, 1988).

Getting to know our real roots means that we must necessarily release any romantic views of our families (Hanson & Bozett, 1985). Our families are essentially serious business (Gross, 1985). We need them, and our responsibility is to create circumstances that make our family bonds both tolerable and reasonably enjoyable (Kreppner & Lerner, 1989).

Leaving our families is usually a constructive move only when we find ourselves in life-threatening circumstances. If we move completely away from our families merely because we are in search of the good life, we will predictably be unable to find what we really want (Kluckhohn & Strodtbeck, 1961). However, realizing that we can be more fulfilled through continued interaction with our families may eventually give us the freedom necessary to develop our own goals and make greater contributions to society (Hoerning & Schaeffer, 1984).

During the course of our lives we must prepare for farewells because of the stark predictability of death. Our challenge is to live as fully as we can until we die. At the same time we need to try to resist tendencies to allow illness, or fears of death, to define and restrict our lives. Understanding how other family members cope with illness and death, and working on changing our beliefs about these life stages, serves to increase our personal freedoms (Goode, 1963).

It is a joy to let go of some of the negative aspects of our lives. We accomplish this partially by first looking at our families objectively, and at ourselves within our families (Gilmour & Duck, 1986). Close scrutiny enables us to come to terms with some of our most burdensome fears and most problematic behaviors (Gilligan, 1982).

None of these strategies are easy to accomplish. In fact, it is extraordinarily difficult to be objective about ourselves. One way to find out who we are in our families is to broaden our contacts with our relatives. For example, when we visit sick or dying relatives, we can more easily discover to what extent our lives reflect theirs and get to know our relatives more deeply. With this experience behind us, a crucial step in further defining ourselves is to decide to change what it is in ourselves that we do not want to be, and to pursue what it is that we want to be.

GREETINGS

In spite of our vital need to free ourselves from our own most unwanted values, we must not spend undue time and energy letting go of burdens or purging ourselves. Physiologically, we must move on and welcome the new if we are to live fully (Gerth & Mills, 1946 and 1953).

As we build our new families today, we need to ask where we are going. Knowing what our families were like in the past is our best starting point, but it is insufficient to know merely where we have come from (Gelfand & Barresi, 1987). Directions in new families depend primarily on where each family member wants to go (Furstenberg & Spanier, 1984).

We must break through the restrictions of closed and isolated family units to welcome more diversity and create new kinds of wholeness. In order to survive, our new families must be sufficiently flexible to accommodate a wide variety of needs, and a wide range of personal preferences (Mead, 1934; Mann, 1988). Above all, it is the quality of relationship flexibility that epitomizes the strength of our new families.

Ideally, new families replace fossilized, authoritarian, hierarchical family structures with flexible, life-oriented, egalitarian relationships (Thorne & Yalmon, 1982). It is through these new flexible structures that we learn to survive by respecting each other, and by perpetuating family bonds that nurture and support us (Teilhard de Chardin, 1965).

New gender definitions are essential components of our new families wherein each family member is as important as the next

(Straus, 1979; Rossi & Rossi, 1990). We cannot continue to burden our children and peers with unrealistic gender expectations, and at the same time be free ourselves (Eggebeen & Uhlenberg, 1985). Our own freedom ultimately depends on others also having freedom (Birren & Bengtson, 1988). In order to move on with our lives as constructively as possible, we must both allow others their freedom and seize our own freedom (Dean et al., 1989).

One advantage of knowing our families' pasts is that we put ourselves into sufficiently secure positions to let go of our own pasts more fully and plunge into unknown futures. In this way we are able to catch up with ourselves; that is, we are no longer pulled back by our pasts.

The future of our visions of new families ultimately rests on what they really are rather than on what we want them to be. It is essential for us to discard family romanticism and recognize that our freedom is necessarily related to our ability to be objective about our significant others. If we are not to be victims of our own family processes in some way, we must create relationships with our families on our terms rather than on our relatives' terms.

The good news is that there is life after traditional or destructive families. We have continuous opportunities to create new kinds of family openness that can adapt effectively to and outlast rapid social changes. Our new families are a true haven–one where deepest needs and yearnings are nurtured–rather than sources of illusion, frustration, and despair. Our hopes can be directed comfortably in these directions since it is only our new family processes and structures that can free us to be who we really are.

Philosophically, however, our raison d'être is not solely to look within our families for fulfillment. Rather, our families are springboards for wider social participation. They enable us to take the quantum leaps we must take in order to give meaningfully to those who are beyond our kin. Our families are essentially our most effective exits and entrances into society. They allow us to make the world a better place for all.

Chapter 16

Answers

To assess whether new families are our most workable and most fulfilling families, some answers are offered to the questions asked at the outset of this study. Although many family themes and patterns described are impressionistic rather than fully substantiated, some of the mutually observed family processes have marked consequences (Cancian, 1987; Kreppner & Lerner, 1989; McAdoo, 1988; Pfeifer & Sussman, 1991; Steinmetz, 1988; Weitzman, 1985).

The answers below are essentially preliminary findings. They can, however, serve as stepping stones toward identifying some of the most significant characteristics of new families, and how we can make our families work for us rather than against us. We must be able to see these possibilities before we can effectively change our lives in these directions (Baltes & Brim, 1980). Because we all need to be released from the automatic, restrictive, inhibiting influences generated by our families (Bowen, 1978), our deliberate acts taken toward freedom within our families will increase our overall freedom.

Although it may not be possible to substantially change what we call human nature in a single generation (Homans, 1961; Mead, 1934; Stack, 1974), some research and clinical findings indicate that widespread shifts in family exchanges are already taking place (Cohler, 1983; Johnson, 1982; Komarovsky, 1962). Furthermore, what we previously thought of as family problems may really be transitions that strengthen the overall functioning of some of our families (Staples, 1986; York, York, & Wachtel, 1982). In new families, individual identity is developed and strengthened through constructive family exchanges. And it is not done in spite of our families or in opposition to them (Mann, 1988).

HOW DO NEW FAMILIES WORK
WELL TOGETHER?

Clinical data suggest that optimally functioning families have flexible relationships. New families are also characterized by emotions that flow smoothly, with cool modes of expression, rather than by emotions that are expressed in hot, intense, fixed patterns. New families work together as a cooperative team whose alliances change as various tasks are performed in daily or yearly routines.

New families are firmly based in this kind of mutually rewarding reciprocity. There is no scapegoating, or unbreachable cut-offs in patterns of family exchanges. New families are characterized by flexible gender roles. Family expectations are sufficiently fluid to be able to promote the growth and well-being of all members rather than a privileged few.

New families have meaningful connections among living generations, with a strong sense of continuity through past generations. The extensive network that characterizes new families serves as a structural and emotional support for their members, especially for their component nuclear units of parents and children. Frequent contacts among family members serve to create and sustain effective, flexible bonding at manageable emotional levels. This prevents intense build-ups that would otherwise inevitably increase family volatility and the possibility of ruptures.

WHAT CAN WE DO TO INCREASE OUR ABILITY
TO ACT CONSTRUCTIVELY IN OUR FAMILIES?

As with participation in all other groups, having a goal clearly in mind helps make an individual's contributions more effective. Predictably, we increase our abilities to effectively act in our families by specifying our objectives and intentions for ourselves and for our behavior toward other family members.

Our understanding of who we are, and who our families are, is our most effective source for constructive action. With adequate self-knowledge and awareness of the nature of our family dependencies, we achieve much more than if we act randomly or blindly. Furthermore, even action aimed at specific goals will not be constructive or effective if it does not have a foundation of knowledge and understanding.

By continuing to work on goals of self-development we become increasingly aware of others' needs as well as our own. As we grow, the outreach of our action widens and we automatically have a more meaningful impact on other family members' lives. We need to work continuously toward our own goals, however, if we are to be truly effective. As soon as we lose our focus, our behavior will become less well-organized, and our priorities and values will be unclear. In order to give our most to others, especially to our families, we have to be fully responsible for working toward goals that are important to our individual fulfillment.

WHAT ARE OUR INDIVIDUAL AND FAMILY RESPONSIBILITIES?

Although they may at least superficially seem to be in competition with each other, our individual and family responsibilities need not be in conflict. Many traditional families sacrifice individuality for the good of the whole, however, whereas nuclear families frequently tend to put individual well-being before family harmony. An intermediate balance of individual and family responsibilities—as in our new families—can and must be achieved if our families are to be strong and healthy.

While our individual responsibilities must include the development of our own strengths and talents, our family responsibilities focus more on trying to meet genuine family needs. These oversimplified definitions and directions cannot afford to imply what we generally know to be selfishness or sacrifice of self. It is the balance or intermediary zone between these opposites that is crucial: only when we keep our primary focus on meeting our own needs are we able to meet our family responsibilities satisfactorily. Also, our abilities to meet our family responsibilities flow from our capacities to meet our individual responsibilities to live fully; that is, according to our own talents and strengths.

Whatever our generational or sibling positions in our families, many of the inevitable tensions between individual and family responsibilities can be resolved by placing a greater emphasis on the need to be fully independent. Paradoxically, we can only be fuller participants in reciprocal family interdependence when we are more complete persons in our own right. This organizational and functional principle operates decisively in all of our families, whatever their ethnic origin, marital structure, or degree of intergenerational connectedness.

HOW CAN WOMEN AND MEN GET ALONG PRODUCTIVELY WITHIN FAMILIES?

New families have flexible divisions of labor where women and men do not necessarily follow cultural dictates for parenting and maintaining the household. This flexibility of division of labor is the foundation of the more viable relationships between women and men that are characteristic of new families.

When women and men are task oriented, they are more likely to be able to get along productively in spite of different needs or varied work styles. Being relatively equally committed to important goals such as child-rearing or maintaining a home results in fewer significant differences or in conflicts being resolved or regulated more or less amicably. Assuming shared responsibilities for family expenses is another critical aspect of the viable give-and-take that characterizes new families.

Under stressful conditions, both women and men tend to fall into stereotypical gender roles. However, when we understand that these patterns are not inevitable and that they can be neutralized, some valuable improvisations can be made in the short or long run. It is in everyone's interest to try to modify conventional cultural expectations for women and men in order to increase family well-being and create new families.

Women and men can improve their relationships with each other by experiencing themselves as whole people within their families rather than as complements to each other. Female and male role complementarity, in fact, suggests a partial development of the strengths and talents of women and men. It is only as more fully developed individuals that they can get along productively, thereby meeting both personal and family needs.

WHAT PREDICTABLE FAMILY CONFLICTS MUST WE FACE?

New families fight constructively when there is conflict, due to the premium they place on working out their problems. Whenever a family status quo is threatened, however, conflict will be predictable. If spouses change in either personal or public ways, relationships throughout their families are affected. These conflicts are inevitable, as is the relationship disorientation and disorganization that occur during birth, marriage, and death.

Individual growth and development also predictably challenge the most established patterns of any family's dynamics. The more individual family members grow, the more their families will have predictable conflicts. The changing of self means that others will, at least initially, pressure that person to go back to behaving as before. Only when we realize at a deep level that personal growth is supremely important for everyone in the long run will we be able to accept individuals' changes readily and easily.

Family needs and expectations frequently seem to be in conflict with individual goals. When this tension becomes uncomfortable, individual goals should be emphasized more than family objectives. It is only by pursuing and developing individual goals that all family members can become full participants in the whole. Conflicts between family needs and individual goals are resolved most effectively when we enter fully into our own projects and give family expectations secondary importance. It is through cultivating this ability to prioritize goals that members of new families are able to make commitments to society as well as to each other.

Predictable conflicts in day-to-day living are welcomed rather than resisted by members of new families. As a result of this acceptance, these conflicts become opportunities for growth and change, and they manifest themselves more as brief transitions than as long phases of chronic tension. By valuing conflicts as means to achieve more viable levels of cooperation, we become stronger individuals and cultivate new, more durable families.

WHAT SATISFACTIONS AND FULFILLMENTS CAN OUR FAMILIES GIVE US?

As sources of our being, our families hold much meaning, especially with regard to significant aspects of self-knowledge. When we know our family histories and the most typical patterns of interaction that transpired between members of our past generations, we predictably deepen our self-knowledge. By seeing the broader picture of our families, we gain healthy perspectives on our own functioning and inclinations toward others.

When we establish and continue to maintain meaningful relationships with many family members in our intergenerational family systems, we create permanent support networks for ourselves. One of life's greatest satisfactions is a sense of belonging, and family connectedness is one of the most intense modes of belonging that human beings can sustain.

Due to the intensity of the emotional bonding that occurs among family members, especially in nuclear families, all families can, at least potentially, provide their members with some degree of emotional fulfillment. Although we must perpetually assert ourselves in order to benefit from positive rather than negative family emotions, members of new families derive a great deal of meaningful satisfaction from these qualities of participation.

Much individual fulfillment is won through participation in family connectedness. We cannot act in a vacuum, and our families are one of our most significant reference groups. It is as daughter, brother, or other family member that we go out into the world as well as assume responsibilities at home. Ideally, meeting these family responsibilities should ultimately modify existing cultural expectations, our own fulfillment being derived from these complex connections. As human beings, we find it difficult to be fulfilled without some regard for our family origins and family relationships.

HOW CAN WE GIVE THE MOST
TO OUR FAMILIES?

We give the most to our families after our own needs have been met. When all family members fill their individual needs, they are in strong positions to give to their family. We also give the most to our families when we have grown and developed our potential, and when we are autonomous.

A specific and important way in which we can give to our families is to make ourselves available to other family members, especially during crises. Whether these difficult circumstances are accidental or life-cycle occurrences, it is clear that we are most needed when our family interdependencies are upset by major events like job losses, migrations, births, marriages, or deaths.

Since crises have several different stages or phases, our deepest commitment to contribute our resourcefulness at these times essentially turns out to be lifelong. Our families remember those they can count on as well as those who retreat in times of need. The effective day-to-day routines in new families prevent, neutralize, or diminish the inevitable stages in family crises.

Our abilities to make honest and open communications are other forms of giving to our families. Families have to be in touch with reality in order to survive and avoid becoming victims of the family myths and romance that abound in contemporary society. When we communicate with our relatives in meaningful ways, we contribute constructively to the pool of values that support and reinforce our families. By being direct in our personal communications with our closest relatives, we keep our family emotional systems open, viable, and enduring. New families thrive due to the openness of their communication systems.

Another way in which we give to our families is through tolerance of our relatives' differences and acceptance of their needs to grow and be strong in their own ways. Nurturing in new families is based on members' mutual respect for the uniqueness of other family members. Participants in new families enhance each other's growth by generating the space and respect they need to become fully themselves.

HOW WILL NEW FAMILIES SURVIVE
INTO THE FUTURE?

New families are durable because they are flexible. Our most rigid, hierarchical family structures break down in modern society because they cannot withstand contemporary pressures effectively. Furthermore, nuclear families become so fragmented that they lose a sense of belonging to living generations as well as past generations.

New families are able to stay connected across several generations of members, thereby perpetuating strength rather than weakness. Contact with peripheral family members is more viable in new families since these members are not trapped in stereotypical roles or authority relations. Respect for elders flourishes in new families, but this is based on meaningful personal relationships rather than on traditional hierarchical forms of filial piety.

New families endure because they meet individual members' needs for real nurturing and support. Exchanges in new families are characteristically not based on sacrificing self. Rather, these families are made up of people who are whole, well-developed individuals.

New families also endure because human beings need families to survive. To the extent that new families continue to meet our most fundamental human needs, they will last further into the future than traditional extended families or nuclear families, which no longer adapt or function effectively in our rapidly changing society.

*   *   *

These answers shed light on critical distinguishing characteristics of new families and ways in which we can make our families work for us. We have to create our own new families, however, in order to effectively replace our traditional and nuclear families. When we recognize new family processes as a viable option, we increase the probability that we will rise above restrictive family ties and claim these more vital ways of being.

Although all families can support and inspire us to some extent, powerful family forces can also move our lives in negative directions rather than positive ones. We must deliberately choose to create new families if they are to exist and persist. We accomplish this initially by placing a value on them. Only in this way can the pioneering activities of creating new families have sufficient importance and meaning for us. Our new families allow us to forge new gender identities and roles within and through family interaction. Our behavior will then meet our individual needs rather than conform to outmoded cultural stereotypes.

Chapter 17

Conclusions

When we look at the broader picture of family changes in the United States and other highly industrialized societies of the twentieth century, especially since World War II, we can see the emergence of some new kinds of resilient families. Established traditional and nuclear families are being replaced by more hardy, more viable family forms and processes.

These new families are characterized (1) by relatively frequent and meaningful contacts among members of all living generations, and (2) by a shared sense of continuity with past generations. New families also have flexible relationship systems with redefined gender roles and gender expectations.

Contemporary family crises reflect diverse economic, social, and cultural contradictions and changes (Mannheim, 1952; Bellah et al., 1985). However, family processes themselves necessarily continue to be one of the most powerful bases of social organization (Rubin, 1976 and 1983). When we consider the ways in which society could or should be changed (Lee, 1955), we must take into account the fact that, for many people, even relatively slight modifications in their families would necessitate dramatic reorientations and reorganizations in their daily lives (Ackerman, 1970).

Families continue to function in society as primary sources of our most cherished values, and as essential personal and community reference groups. Families also transmit diverse socially significant meanings to their members throughout their lives (Merton & Kitt, 1969). Even though modern industrial societies may produce many different family forms in the short span of a generation or two

(Mead, 1970), some important continuities in family processes persist through time (Goode, 1963).

Our variety of existing contemporary families can be thought of as evidence for a human evolution that moves toward increasing complexity (Teilhard de Chardin, 1965). Observable and experienced family contrasts prompt us to rethink and redefine our definitions and understanding of families (Thorne & Yalmon, 1982; Schur, 1971; Slater, 1991). Accounts of minority group experiences (Billingsley, 1968), as well as longitudinal research findings from studies of divorce and remarriage (Beal & Hochman, 1991; Cherlin, 1981; Wallerstein & Kelly, 1980), necessarily broaden our perspectives and assumptions about family changes. Furthermore, unless we broaden our habitual understanding of our families, we cannot be ready and willing to create new families (Young & Wilmott, 1973; Sampson, 1988). For example, only when we successfully modify our traditional or conventional gender role patterns will we be able to understand ourselves more adequately, survive more effectively, and increase the possibilities of being fulfilled (Eggebeen & Uhlenberg, 1985; Lewis & Sussman, 1986).

Family theories provide our most useful means for assessing the strengths and weaknesses of family functioning. Clinical and research data that have been collected and organized around the concepts of family theories enable us to separate reality from mythology and formulate effective strategies for creating changes within and between families (Bagarozzi & Anderson, 1989).

The following generalizations and propositions about new families are intended to contribute toward the further development of family theories. Emphasis here is given to new families so that optimal conditions for nurturance can be stated in objective rather than subjective or moralistic terms.

Although much substantiation is still required for any of these generalizations and propositions to be fully integrated in the form of family theories, the observations and ideas outlined below are intended to move us toward that goal. Reliable family theories can only be realistically developed when the most significant and enduring aspects of family relationships and patterns of family interaction are accurately conceptualized and understood.

GENERALIZATIONS

1. New families have specific structural and interactional characteristics that allow them to survive and thrive more effectively than traditional extended and modern nuclear families.
2. New families have flexible relationship systems based on redefined gender role expectations and reinterpreted gender responsibilities.
3. Traditional divisions of labor in extended and nuclear families are replaced, in new families, by a more fluid give-and-take reciprocity which meets both individual and family needs.
4. Personal growth and development are essential, integral components of new families. Individual maturation processes support and strengthen rather than threaten the continuity of new families.
5. New families consistently and predictably work for us instead of against us. Their viability ultimately depends on our abilities to continue to grow and develop.
6. New families emerge in all segments of the population. They are evolutionary adaptations that go beyond any particular social class, ethnic group, or nation.
7. The capacity to share some of the same goals perpetuates new families' continuities and enables their members to interact cooperatively rather than competitively. These qualities of ongoing intergenerational contacts help new families' individual members to transcend many of the immediate conflicts and stresses that are necessarily associated with everyday life.
8. Knowing the characteristics and possibilities of new families enables us to work more effectively toward achieving such optimal conditions in our own lives.

PROPOSITIONS

1. New families will survive further into the future than either traditional extended families or modern nuclear families.
2. New families, with characteristically flexible relationship systems and fluid gender role definitions, are more able to meet

their individual members' needs than traditional and nuclear families, which have less flexible relationship systems and less fluid gender role definitions.

3. Optimal functioning occurs in new families because of their greater relationship system flexibility and versatility.

4. New families provide more tolerance and more support for their members' personal growth than traditional or nuclear families.

5. To the extent that we continue to grow and develop our individual strengths and talents in autonomous ways, and at the same time stay in meaningful contact with our families, new families will perpetuate themselves.

6. Although new families make up a relatively small proportion of all families, they are distributed evenly among all social classes, ethnic groups, and nation-states.

7. New families are characterized by more effective survival and life-satisfaction activities than can be found in traditional or nuclear families. The cooperation and support that characterize new families result from the frequency of meaningful contacts among members of different generations.

8. The more we are able to learn what new families are like, the greater the probability we will be able to emulate and sustain these freer forms and processes of family living.

Although new families comprise only a relatively small group of families who are successfully pioneering more viable ways to survive and be fulfilled, they have the power, by example, to show us some of the ways we can make our families work for us more satisfactorily. This knowledge decreases the likelihood that we will experience inordinately tragic family circumstances such as the commonly shared experience of family members who care deeply about each other severing ties because they are unable to tolerate or come to terms with their differences. On a more positive note, new families show us how to deal satisfactorily with our everyday needs for intimacy and for contributing constructively to society as well as our families.

In our current social conditions, where dual-earner families are the norm, we must be able to discern which specific family structures and processes, and which patterns of accomplishing tasks, are more viable than others. For example, the evidence from different kinds of family functioning suggests that our new single-parent families are less burdened by the family and social pressures that generally characterize other single-parent families or traditional and nuclear families.

Both single-parent and dual-parent new families provide us with solutions for coping with everyday realities. The experiences of single-parent and dual-parent new families relieve us of the need to become further immobilized by problems and dissatisfactions related to family living. In order to strengthen and perpetuate these positive influences, however, we must increase our numbers of new families. We do this by making sure that as many people as possible can follow their discoveries of strengths, capabilities, and enlightenment. If our new families could become the norm and expectation of most people, our communities and nations would be stronger and more viable. New families move us toward a healthy and prosperous future which brings with it increased individual and social fulfillment for all.

Appendix

Summary information about the major substantive origins and formative background influences of *New Families: Reviving and Creating Meaningful Bonds* is given in the following sections: data sources, theoretical orientation, methodology, and literature reviews. Hypothetical statements about a wide range of different family characteristics are also presented in the form of ideal types for a traditional family, a nuclear family and a new family. These representative summations appear in the final section of the appendix.

DATA SOURCES

The life history data used as the primary basis for all the generalizations and propositions in this book derive mainly from my professional experience: 22 years of private practice as a family therapist and five years as a family therapist and clinical consultant for Frederick County Community Mental Health Services, Frederick, MD. These clinical applications, which consistently yield compelling life history materials, are complemented by research data collected from several interview projects conducted at Georgetown University during the same 22-year period.

Life history data from more than five years of experience in organizing women's empowerment discussion groups in the Washington, DC, area have also been used. Even though a wide range of topics is typically examined during these exchanges among women, family stresses and related personal experiences are persistent central concerns. These discussions frequently include the participants' observations about both women's and men's contributions and stresses in relation to families and wider society.

THEORETICAL ORIENTATION

The book is wholly based on identity empowerment theory–a clinical perspective that I developed within the subdiscipline of clinical sociology (Hall, 1989, 1990, 1991, and 1992). Identity empowerment theory consists of ten basic sociological concepts–self, dyad, triad, family, religion, definition of the situation, reference group, class, culture, and society–that describe and explain significant links among different aspects of interdependency. The ten concepts of identity empowerment theory synthesize microsociological and macrosociological dimensions of individuals and society, as well as subjective and objective aspects of interpersonal experience, world views, and social structures. *New Families: Reviving and Creating Meaningful Bonds* describes specific necessary conditions for new families, families which support the optimum identity empowerment of all family members.

The main theses of this book partially derive from Murray Bowen's family systems theory (Bowen, 1978; Hall, 1981; Kerr & Bowen, 1988), which has been adapted here as a critical component of identity empowerment theory. Bowen's family systems theory consists of eight basic concepts–differentiation of self, triangles, nuclear family emotional system, sibling position, family projection process, multigenerational process, emotional cut-off, and emotional process in society–that describe and explain emotional dependence and reactivity in families and other kinds of human relationship systems. Bowen's definition of families as emotional systems provides a useful view of the strengths and weaknesses in human relationships, individuation processes, and evolutionary adaptations.

METHODOLOGY

Repeated clinical interviews, as well as research interviews with families, were the primary means used to collect data about family members from three generations of the same families. Hard facts–birth dates, death dates, cause of death, marriage dates, divorce dates, migrations, occupations, and state of health–were documented in the different interview settings. Also documented were assessments about the qualities and intensities of dependence among all three generations of the same family members. Conflictual or affectionate exchanges, and relationships that are emotionally or geographically distant such as cut-offs between different generations or between siblings, were also noted. The complex information recorded was diagrammed wherever possible so that patterns and repetitions in family events among different generations could be identified more clearly.

These schemas and strategies for accumulating family data combined to give relatively holistic profiles of family interaction. Observations of interactions during clinical exchanges, as well as family members' reports and anecdotes about each other, yielded rich details about the everyday behavior characteristic of these families.

Most of the clinical interventions and research conducted consisted of question-and-answer exchanges between therapist and client or researcher and subject, together with guided or open-ended reflections and deliberations about the nature of individual and shared experiences within the different families. This methodology increased clients' and subjects' abilities to make assessments about significant subjective and objective dimensions of their own families' lives, especially when selected probe and follow-up questions were used in the exchanges. Continued meetings and contacts with the same families over months, and sometimes years, made the collection of longitudinal data feasible. Furthermore, the therapist's relative objectivity and ability to verify data increased as family members returned for continued consultations.

Although the fact that most of the families interviewed originally experienced some kind of problem inevitably skews the representativeness of these data, one offsetting advantage is that it is generally during crises that the vital infrastructures of families are seen most clearly. Clinical interventions provide valuable opportunities for the observation of families as they really are, with all their taken-for-granted assumptions revealed, and not as we or they want them to be.

LITERATURE REVIEWS

To some extent this book resulted from reviews and analyses of sociological and behavioral research projects that describe and explain emotional connectedness and relationships among different generations (Aldous & Hill, 1965; Mutran & Reitzes, 1984), family interdependencies (Cohler, 1983; Caplow, 1968; Cooley, 1964; Pruitt, 1981), family influences on subjective development (Fein, 1988; Glassner & Freedman, 1979; Guerin, 1976; Stryker, 1968;

Rosenberg & Kaplan, 1982), and family transitions (Skolnick & Skolnick, 1989; Walsh, 1982). Particular attention is paid to gender issues within families and in society at large (Walters et al., 1988), as well as to the impact of broad social influences on families (Caute, 1967; Dahrendorf, 1959; Darwin, 1964; Durkheim, 1951; Engels, 1955; Gerth & Mills, 1946; Mead, 1934; Mills, 1959; Parsons, 1951; Simmel, 1950; Thomas, 1931; Thomas & Znaniecki, 1927; von Bertalanffy, 1968).

New Families: Reviving and Creating Meaningful Bonds goes beyond these particular topics to include reviews of research that describe and explain circumstances characteristic of varied social classes, ethnic groups, and family types, especially those found in contemporary U.S. society. This book fills a gap in existing research on family interaction by specifying some of the optimal conditions for achieving meaningful and satisfying lives through the creation of new families within diverse social classes and ethnic groups.

IDEAL TYPES

An ideal type profile is a description or summary statement about a particular subject that is based on information abstracted from facts and observations of reality. This methodological tool is intended to represent the essence of a specific phenomenon.

Ideal type profiles of essential distinguishing characteristics from traditional, nuclear, and new families are presented below. These descriptions clarify some of the meanings given to selected substantive themes and analyses discussed throughout *New Families: Reviving and Creating Meaningful Bonds.*

The properties of traditional, nuclear, and new families specified in these ideal types are not formally correlated with statistical norms or averages. In fact, in contrast to traditional and nuclear families, new families are an emergent minority of families that are found in all social classes and ethnic groups. However, due to the fact that the trends and distinguishing traits of traditional, nuclear, and new families appear throughout the general population, it is this pervasiveness of their characteristic patterns of behavior which ultimately allows for the following generalizations and propositions.

Traditional Families

1. Traditional families are found in most social classes and ethnic groups in most societies.
2. Traditional families are based on hierarchical authority structures which have relatively ritualistic exchanges among family members at different generational levels.
3. Traditional families have relatively rigid gender and age roles and expectations, and family members' behavior in these families tends to conform fairly closely to cultural stereotypes.
4. Traditional families have relatively closed relationship systems with dependencies that show fixed and static characteristics. These conditions impede the growth and creativity of many of their family members who cannot become strong in their own right through expressing their own personal values and principles.
5. Traditional families have relatively fixed belief systems which generally inhibit or control their members' attitudes and activities.
6. Traditional families have strong authority structures. These hierarchical structures usually define only one head of family in two-parent families.
7. Traditional families have relatively exclusive relationship systems. They may include members of older generations and ancestors, but they may also exclude relatives who do not conform to current family members' expectations.
8. Traditional families are frequently imbalanced by cut-offs in their relationship systems. Segments of traditional families that are stressed frequently withdraw from the rest of the family and even from society, essentially living in a world of their own.

Nuclear Families

1. Nuclear families are found in most social classes and most ethnic groups in contemporary industrial societies.
2. Nuclear families are based on miniature hierarchical authority structures–between one or two parents at one generational level and one or more children at the other generational level–

which contain relatively few exchanges with older family members.

3. Nuclear families have clearly defined conventional gender and age roles and expectations, and family members' behavior tends to conform to cultural stereotypes for modern families.

4. Nuclear families are frequently fragmented by divorce and other kinds of separations. Consequently, they create extremely intense interdependent relationship systems. These nuclear family dependencies are frequently fixed in repetitive patterns, and family members have difficulty growing creatively and in accordance with their own values and principles.

5. Nuclear families usually have clearly pronounced belief systems which strongly influence and control their members' attitudes and activities.

6. Nuclear families have authority structures that tend to define only one head of family in each two-parent family.

7. The fragmented, intense relationship systems of nuclear families are frequently cut off from older generations and ancestors.

8. Nuclear families are frequently imbalanced by cut-offs in their relationship systems. Consequently, they may withdraw from their kin groups and the rest of society, conducting their everyday lives in relative isolation, especially from other family members.

New Families

1. Although new families are significantly fewer in number than traditional or nuclear families, they are found in all social classes and all ethnic groups in contemporary industrial societies.

2. New families are distinctive in that they have more active, ongoing exchanges among their different generations than traditional or nuclear families.

3. New families have more fluid gender and age roles and expectations than traditional or nuclear families, with the result that family members' behaviors go beyond cultural stereotypes and conventional expectations.

4. New families have flexible and open relationship systems, whose dependencies are rarely fixed or static. These condi-

tions nurture the growth and creativity of all family members and allow them to become strong according to their own values and principles.

5. New families have flexible belief systems that consistently support their members' attitudes and activities rather than inhibiting or controlling them.

6. New families have minimal authority structures. New families that have two parents are symmetrically balanced (with two heads of family) rather than hierarchical (with one head of family), as is typical of two-parent traditional and nuclear families.

7. New families have more open, inclusive relationship systems than traditional or nuclear families. They actively incorporate as many relatives as possible from older and lateral generations, pulling family members into their emotional systems from the further reaches of their kin networks.

8. New families are more balanced and more integrated than traditional and nuclear families, which tend to be fragmented or cut off from other parts of their families or from society itself. Thus new families function as viable wholes in their own right and have vital connections to their respective community and social settings.

References

Ackerman, N.W. 1970. *Family Therapy in Transition*. Boston: Little, Brown.

Ackerman, N.W. 1958. *The Psychodynamics of Family Life*. New York: Basic Books.

Adams, B.N. 1968. *Kinship in an Urban Setting*. Chicago: Markham.

Aldous, J. 1987. "Family life of the elderly and near-elderly." *Journal of Marriage and the Family, 49*, 227-234.

Aldous, J. & Hill, R. 1965. "Social cohesion, lineage type and intergenerational transmission." *Social Forces, 43*, 471-482.

Anderson, T.B. 1984. "Widowhood as a life transition: Its impact on kinship ties." *Journal of Marriage and the Family, 46*, 105-114.

Angell, R.C. [1936] 1965. *The Family Encounters the Depression*. Gloucester, MA: Peter Smith.

Arcana, J. 1986. *Every Mother's Son: The Role of Mothers in the Making of Men*. Seattle: The Seal Press.

Aries, P. 1962. *Centuries of Childhood: A Social History of Family Life* (R. Baddick, Trans.). New York: Knopf.

Atkinson, M.P., Kivett, V.R., & Campbell, R.T. 1986. "Intergenerational solidarity: An examination of a theoretical model." *Journal of Gerontology, 41*, 408-416.

Bagarozzi, D.A. & Anderson, S.A. 1989. *Personal, Marital, and Family Myths: Theoretical Formulations and Clinical Strategies*. New York: W.W. Norton.

Baltes, P.B. & Brim, O.G., Jr. (Eds.). 1980. *Life-Span Development and Behavior*. New York: Academic Press.

Baruch, G. & Barnett, R.C. 1983. "Adult daughters' relationships with their mothers." *Journal of Marriage and the Family, 45*, 601-606.

Beal, E. & Hochman, G. 1991. *The Adult Children of Divorce*. New York: Delacorte.

Becker, H. 1963. *Outsiders: Studies in the Sociology of Deviance*. New York: Free Press.

Bellah, R., Madsen, R., Sullivan, W.M., Swidler, A., & Tipton, S.M. 1985. *Habits of the Heart: Individualism and Commitment in American Life*. Berkeley, CA: University of California Press.

Bengtson, V.L. 1975. "Generation and family effects in value socialization." *American Sociological Review, 40*, 358-371.

Bengtson, V.L. & Robertson, J.F. (Eds.). 1985. *Grandparenthood*. Beverly Hills, CA: Sage.

Benson, L. 1968. *Fatherhood: A Sociological Perspective*. New York: Random House.

Berger, P.L. & Kellner, H. 1977. "Marriage and the construction of reality." In *Facing Up to Modernity*, edited by P.L. Berger. (pp. 5-22). New York: Basic Books.

Berger, P.L. & Luckmann, T. 1966. *The Social Construction of Reality: A Treatise in the Sociology of Knowledge.* New York: Doubleday.

Bernard, J. 1974. *The Future of Motherhood.* New York: The Dial Press.

Bettelheim, B. 1987. *A Good Enough Parent.* New York: Knopf.

Bettelheim, B. 1962. "The problem of generations." *Daedalus, 91,* 68-96.

Beutler, I.F., Burr, W.R., Bahr, K.S., & Herrin, D.A. 1989. "The family realm: Theoretical contributions for understanding its consequences." *Journal of Marriage and the Family, 51,* 805-816.

Billingsley, A. 1968. *Black Families in White America.* Englewood Cliffs, NJ: Prentice-Hall.

Birren, J.E. & Bengtson, V.L. (Eds.). 1988. *Emergent Theories of Aging.* New York: Springer.

Blau, P.M. 1964. *Exchange and Power in Social Life.* New York: John Wiley.

Bloomfield, H.H. 1983. *Making Peace with Your Parents: The Key to Enriching Your Life and All Your Relationships.* New York: Random House.

Blumer, H. 1969. *Symbolic Interaction: Perspective and Method.* Englewood Cliffs, NJ: Prentice-Hall.

Blumstein, P. & Schwartz, P. 1983. *American Couples.* Fairfield, NJ: William Morrow.

Boszormenyi-Nagy, I. & Framo, J. (Eds.). 1965. *Intensive Family Therapy.* New York: Harper & Row.

Bowen, M. 1978. *Family Therapy in Clinical Practice.* New York: Aronson.

Boyd, C.J. 1989. "Mothers and daughters: A discussion of theory and research." *Journal of Marriage and the Family, 51,* 291-302.

Brody, E.M., Hoffman, C., Kleban, M.H., & Schoonover, C.B. 1989. "Caregiving daughters and their local siblings: Perceptions, strains and interactions." *The Gerontologist, 29,* 529-538.

Buunk, B. and Van Driel, B. 1989. *Variant Lifestyles and Relationships.* Newbury Park, CA: Sage.

Cancian, F.M. 1987. *Love in America: Gender and Self-Development.* Cambridge, MA: Cambridge University Press.

Caplan, P.J. 1989. *Don't Blame Mother: Mending the Mother-Daughter Relationship.* New York: Harper & Row.

Caplow, T. 1968. *Two Against One: Coalitions in Triads.* Englewood Cliffs, NJ: Prentice-Hall.

Carlson, A.C. 1990. *The Swedish Experiment in Family Politics: The Myrdals and the Interwar Population Crisis.* New Brunswick, NJ: Rutgers University Press.

Carlson, C. 1990. *Perspectives on the Family: History, Class, and Feminism.* Belmont, CA: Wadsworth.

Cates, J. & Sussman, M.B. 1982. *Family Systems and Inheritance.* New York: The Haworth Press.

Caute, D. (Ed.). 1967. *Essential Writings of Karl Marx.* New York: Collier.

Cheal, D.J. 1983. "Intergenerational family transfers." *Journal of Marriage and the Family, 45,* 805-813.

Cherlin, A.J. 1988. *The Changing American Family and Public Policy.* Washington, DC: The Urban Institute Press.

Cherlin, A.J. 1981. *Marriage, Divorce and Remarriage.* Cambridge, MA: Harvard University Press.

Chess, S. & Thomas, A. 1986. *Temperament in Clinical Practice.* New York: Guilford Press.

Chodorow, N. 1978. *The Reproduction of Mothering: Psychoanalysis and the Sociology of Gender.* Berkeley: University of California Press.

Christiansen, H.T. (Ed.). 1964. *Handbook of Marriage and the Family.* Chicago: Rand-McNally.

Cicirelli, V.G. 1983. "Adult children's attachment and helping behavior to elderly parents: A path model." *Journal of Marriage and the Family, 45,* 815-823.

Clavan, S. 1978. "The impact of social class and social trends on the role of grandparents." *The Family Coordinator, 27,* 351-357.

Cohler, B. 1983. "Autonomy and interdependence in the family of adulthood: A psychological perspective." *The Gerontologist, 23,* 33-40.

Cohler, B. & Grunebaum, H. 1981. *Mothers, Grandmothers, and Daughters: Personality and Childcare in Three-Generation Families.* New York: Wiley.

Colleta, N.D. & Lee, D. 1983. "The impact of support for black adolescent mothers." *Journal of Family Issues, 4,* 127-143.

Cooley, C.H. [1902] 1964. *Human Nature and the Social Order.* New York: Schocken.

Dahrendorf, R. 1959. *Class and Class Conflict in Industrial Society.* Stanford, CA: Stanford University Press.

Dally, A. 1982. *Inventing Motherhood: The Consequences of an Ideal.* New York: Schocken.

D'Antonio, W.V. & Aldous, J. (Eds.). 1983. *Families and Religions: Conflict and Change in Modern Society.* Beverly Hills, CA: Sage.

Darwin, C.R. [1859] 1964. *On the Origin of Species.* Cambridge, MA: Harvard University Press.

Dean, A., Kolody, B., Wood, P., & Ensel, W.M. 1989. "Measuring the communication of social support from adult children." *Journal of Gerontology, 44,* 71-79.

de Beauvoir, S. [1949] 1974. *The Second Sex.* New York: Vintage.

Dinnerstein, D. 1977. *The Mermaid and the Minotaur.* New York: Harper & Row.

Dizard, J.E. & Gadlin, H. 1990. *The Minimal Family.* Amherst, MA: University of Massachusetts Press.

Dornbusch, S.M. & Strober, M.H. (Eds.). 1988. *Feminism, Children, and the New Families.* New York: Guilford Press.

Dunn, J. 1985. *Sisters and Brothers.* Cambridge, MA: Harvard University Press.

Durkheim, E. [1897] 1951. *Suicide* (Trans. J. Spaulding & G. Simpson). New York: Free Press.

Eggebeen, D. & Uhlenberg, P. 1985. "Changes in the organization of men's lives: 1960-1980." *Family Relations, 34,* 251-257.

Elder, G.H., Jr. & Clipp, E. 1988. "War experience and social ties: Influences across 40 years in men's lives." In *Social Structures and Human Lives,* edited by M.W. Riley. (pp. 306-327). Newbury Park, CA: Sage.

Engels, F. [1884] 1955. *The Origin of the Family, Private Property and the State.* Moscow: Foreign Language Publishing House.

Falicov, C.J. (Ed.). 1988. *Family Transitions: Continuity and Change Over the Life Cycle.* New York: Guilford Press.

Farber, B. 1973. *Family and Kinship in Modern Society.* Glenview, IL: Scott, Foresman.

Farrell, W. 1974. *The Liberated Man.* New York: Random House.

Fein, M.L. 1988. "Resocialization: A neglected paradigm." *Clinical Sociology Review, 6,* 88-100.

Ferree, M.M. 1990. "Feminism and family research." *Journal of Marriage and the Family, 52,* 844-866.

Finley, N.J. 1989. "Gender differences in caregiving for elderly parents." *Journal of Marriage and the Family, 51,* 79-86.

Fischer, L.R. 1986. "Married men and their mothers." *Journal of Comparative Family Studies, 14,* 393-402.

Fischer, L.R. 1981. "Transitions in the mother-daughter relationship." *Journal of Marriage and the Family, 43,* 613-622.

Frazier, E.F. 1939. *The Negro Family in the United States.* Chicago: Chicago University Press.

Freud, S. [1930] 1958. *Civilization and Its Discontents.* New York: Doubleday-Anchor.

Friedman, E.H. 1985. Generation to Generation: Family Process in Church and Synagogue. New York: Guilford Press.

Furstenberg, F.F., Jr. & Spanier, G.B. 1984. *Recycling the Family: Remarriage after Divorce.* Beverly Hills, CA: Sage.

Galambos, N.L. & Silbereisen, R.K. 1989. "Role strain in West German dual-earner households." *Journal of Marriage and the Family, 51,* 385-390.

Garfinkel, H. 1967. *Studies in Ethnomethodology.* Englewood Cliffs, NJ: Prentice-Hall.

Gelfand, D.E. & Barresi, C.M. (Eds.). 1987. *Ethnic Dimensions of Aging.* New York: Springer.

Gelles, R.J. & Cornell, C.P. (Eds.). 1990. *Intimate Violence in Families.* Newbury Park, CA: Sage.

Gerth, H. & Mills, C.W. 1953. *Character and Social Structure: The Psychology of Social Institutions.* New York: Harcourt, Brace, and World.

Gerth, H. & Mills, C.W. 1946. *From Max Weber: Essays in Sociology.* New York: Oxford University Press.

Gil, D. 1970. *Violence Against Children.* Cambridge, MA: Harvard University Press.

Gilligan, C. 1982. *In a Different Voice: Psychological Theory and Women's Development.* Cambridge, MA: Harvard University Press.

Gilmour, R. & Duck, S. (Eds.). 1986. *The Emerging Field of Personal Relationships.* Hillsdale, NJ: Lawrence Erlbaum.

Glass, J., Bengtson, V.L., & Dunham, C.C. 1986. "Attitude similarity in three-generation families: Socialization, status inheritance, or reciprocal influence?" *American Sociological Review, 51*, 685-698.

Glassner, B. & Freedman, J. 1979. *Clinical Sociology.* New York: Longman.

Goffman, E. 1959. *The Presentation of Self in Everyday Life.* New York: Doubleday.

Goode, W.J. 1963. *World Revolution and Family Patterns.* New York: Free Press.

Goode, W.J. 1956. *After Divorce.* New York: Macmillan.

Goody, J.R. 1962. *Death, Property and the Ancestors.* Stanford, CA: Stanford University Press.

Gross, Z.H. 1985. *And You Thought It Was All Over! Mothers and Their Adult Children.* New York: St. Martin's Press.

Guerin, P.J. (Ed.). 1976. *Family Therapy.* New York: Gardner Press.

Haley, J. 1976. *Problem-Solving Therapy.* San Francisco: Jossey-Bass.

Halford, W.K., Hahlweg, K., & Dunne, M. 1990. "Cross-cultural study of marital communication and marital distress." *Journal of Marriage and the Family, 52*, 487-500.

Hall, C.M. 1992. "Struggle for autonomy." *Sociological Practice Review, 3*, 16-22.

Hall, C.M. 1991. "Clinical sociology and religion." *Clinical Sociology Review, 9*, 48-58.

Hall, C.M. 1990. "Identity empowerment through clinical sociology." *Clinical Sociology Review, 8*, 69-86.

Hall, C.M. 1989. "Triadic analysis: A conceptual tool for clinical sociologists." *Clinical Sociology Review, 7*, 97-110.

Hall, C.M. 1981. *The Bowen Family Theory and Its Uses.* New York: Aronson.

Hampton, R.L. (Ed.). 1987. *Violence in the Black Family: Correlates and Consequences.* Lexington, MA: Lexington Books.

Hanscombe, G. & Forster, J. 1982. *Rocking the Cradle: Lesbian Mothers, A Challenge in Family Living.* Boston: Alyson.

Hanson, S. & Bozett, F. 1985. *Dimensions of Fatherhood.* Beverly Hills, CA: Sage.

Hays, W. & Mindel, C.H. 1973. "Extended kinship relations in black and white families." *Journal of Marriage and the Family, 35*, 51-56.

Hill, R. 1949. *Families Under Stress.* New York: Harper & Row.

Hill, R., Foote, N., Aldous, J., Carlson, R., & MacDonald, R. 1970. *Family Development in Three Generations.* Cambridge, MA: Schenkman.

Hoerning, E.M. & Schaeffer, D. (Eds.). 1984. *Intergenerational Relationships.* Lewiston, NY: C.J. Hogrete.

Homans, G. 1961. *Social Behavior: Its Elementary Forms.* New York: Harcourt, Brace, and World.

Hurvitz, N. 1979. "The sociologist as a marital and family therapist." *American Behavioral Scientist, 22,* 557-576.

Hutchings, N. 1988. *The Violent Family: Victimization of Women, Children, and Elders.* New York: Human Sciences Press.

Iutcovich, J.M. & Iutcovich, M. (Eds.). 1987. *The Sociologist as Consultant.* New York: Praeger.

Jackson, D.D. (Ed.). 1968a. *Therapy, Communication and Change.* Palo Alto, CA: Science and Behavior Books.

Jackson, D.D. (Ed.). 1968b. *Communication, Family and Marriage.* Palo Alto, CA: Science and Behavior Books.

Johnson, C.L. 1988. *Ex Familia: Grandparents, Parents, and Children Adjust to Divorce.* New Brunswick: Rutgers University Press.

Johnson, C.L. 1982. "Sibling solidarity: Its origin and functioning in Italian-American families." *Journal of Marriage and the Family, 44,* 155-167.

Johnson, C.L. & Barer, B.M. 1987. "Marital instability and the changing kinship networks of grandparents." *The Gerontologist, 27,* 330-335.

Johnson, M.M. 1988. *Strong Mothers, Weak Wives: The Search for Gender Equality.* Berkeley: University of California Press.

Kassop, M. 1987. "Salvador Minuchin: A sociological analysis of his family therapy theory." *Clinical Sociology Review, 5,* 158-167.

Keniston, K. 1965. *The Uncommitted: Alienated Youth in American Society.* New York: Harcourt, Brace, and World.

Kerr, M. & Bowen, M. 1988. *Family Evaluation–An Approach Based on Bowen Theory.* New York: W.W. Norton.

Kingson, E.R., Hirshorn, B.A., & Cornman, J.M. 1986. *Ties That Bond: The Interdependence of Generations.* Cabin John, MD: Seven Locks Press.

Kinsey, A.C., Pomeroy, W.B., & Martin, C.E. 1953. *Sexual Behavior in the Human Female.* Philadelphia: W.B. Saunders.

Kinsey, A.C., Pomeroy, W.B., & Martin, C.E. 1948. *Sexual Behavior in the Human Male.* Philadelphia: W.B. Saunders.

Kivett, V.R. 1985. "Grandfathers and grandchildren: Patterns of association, helping, and psychological closeness." *Family Relations, 34,* 565-571.

Klein, D.M. & Aldous, J. (Eds.). 1988. *Social Stress and Family Development.* New York: Guilford Press.

Kluckhohn, F.R. & Strodtbeck, F.L. 1961. *Variations in Value Orientations.* Evanston, IL: Row, Peterson.

Komarovsky, M. 1962. *Blue Collar Marriage.* New York: Vintage.

Koos, E.L. [1946] 1973. *Families in Trouble.* New York: Russell & Russell.

Kreppner, K. & Lerner, R.M. (Eds.). 1989. *Family Systems and Life-Span Development.* Hillsdale, NJ: Lawrence Erlbaum.

Laing, R.D. 1971. *The Politics of the Family.* New York: Random House.

Lamb, M. 1987. *The Father's Role: Cross-Cultural Perspectives.* Hillsdale, NJ: Lawrence Erlbaum.

Lee, A.M. 1955. "The clinical study of society." *American Sociological Review, 20,* 648-653.

Lee, G.R. 1980. "Kinship in the seventies: A decade review of research and theory." *Journal of Marriage and the Family*, *42*, 923-934.

Lee, G.R. & Ellithorpe, E. 1982. "Intergenerational exchange and subjective well-being among the elderly." *Journal of Marriage and the Family*, *44*, 217-224.

Leonard, L.S. 1983. *The Wounded Woman: Healing the Father-Daughter Relationship*. Boulder, CO: Shambhala.

Levinson, D. 1989. *Family Violence in Cross-Cultural Perspective*. Newbury Park, CA: Sage.

Levinson, D.J. 1978. *The Seasons of a Man's Life*. New York: Vintage.

Levitan, S.A., Belous, R. S. and Gallo, F. 1988. *What's Happening to the American Family? Tensions, Hopes, Realities*. Baltimore, MD: Johns Hopkins University Press.

Lewis, M. (Ed.). 1982. *Beyond the Dyad*. New York: Plenum.

Lewis, R. & Sussman, M.B. (Eds.). 1986. *Men's Changing Roles in the Family*. New York: The Haworth Press.

Liebow, E. 1966. *Tally's Corner*. Boston: Little, Brown.

Luster, T., Rhoades, K., & Haas, B. 1989. "Relation between parental values and parenting behavior." *Journal of Marriage and the Family*, *51*, 139-148.

Lynn, D. 1974. *The Father: His Role in Child Development*. Belmont, CA: Wadsworth.

Madanes, C. 1981. *Strategic Family Therapy*. San Francisco: Jossey-Bass.

Mangen, D.J., Bengtson, V.L., & Landry, P.H. 1988. *Measurement of Intergenerational Relations*. Beverly Hills, CA: Sage.

Mann, P.S. 1988. "Personal identity matters." *Social Theory & Practice*, *14*, 285-316.

Mannheim, K. 1952. "The problem of generations." In *Essays on the Sociology of Knowledge*, edited by K. Mannheim. London: Routledge & Kegan Paul.

Maslow, A. 1976. *Religions, Values and Peak Experiences*. New York: Penguin.

McAdoo, H. (Ed.). 1988. *Black Families*. Beverly Hills, CA: Sage.

McGoldrick, M., Pearce, J.K., & Giordano, J. (Eds.) 1982. *Ethnicity and Family Therapy*. New York: Guilford Press.

McNeely, R.L. & Colen, J.L. (Eds.). 1983. *Aging in Minority Groups*. Beverly Hills, CA: Sage.

Mead, G.H. 1934. *Mind, Self and Society*. Chicago: University of Chicago Press.

Mead, M. 1970. *Culture and Commitment: A Study of the Generation Gap*. Garden City, NY: Natural History Press/Doubleday.

Merton, R.K. & Kitt, A.S. 1969. "Reference groups." In *Sociological Theory*, edited by L.A. Coser and B. Rosenberg. (pp. 243-250). New York: Macmillan.

Milardo, R.W. (Ed.). 1988. *Families and Social Networks*. Newbury Park, CA: Sage.

Mills, C.W. 1959. *The Sociological Imagination*. London: Oxford University Press.

Mills, C.W. 1956. *The Power Elite*. London: Oxford University Press.

Mindel, C.H., Habenstein, R.W., & Wright, R. (Eds.). 1988. *Ethnic Families in America: Patterns and Variations*. New York: Elsevier.

Minuchin, S. 1974. *Families and Family Therapy*. Cambridge, MA: Harvard University Press.

Minuchin, S. & Fishman, H.C. 1981. *Family Therapy Techniques*. Cambridge, MA: Harvard University Press.

Morris, D. 1967. *The Naked Ape*. London: Jonathan Cape, 1967.

Mutran, E. & Reitzes, D.C. 1984. "Intergenerational support activities and well-being among the elderly: A convergence of exchange and symbolic interaction perspectives." *American Sociological Review, 49*, 117-130.

Nelson, M.K. 1990. *Negotiated Care: The Experience of Family Day Care Providers*. Philadelphia, PA: Temple University Press.

Papp, P. 1983. *The Process of Change*. New York: Guilford Press.

Parsons, T. 1968. *The Structure of Social Action*. New York: Free Press.

Parsons, T. 1951. *The Social System*. New York: Free Press.

Parsons, T. & Bales, R.F. 1955. *Family Socialization and Interaction Process*. Glencoe, IL: Free Press.

Pfeifer, S.K. & Sussman, M.B. (Eds.). 1991. *Families: Intergenerational and Generational Connections*. New York: The Haworth Press.

Pleck, E.H. 1987. *Domestic Tyranny: The Making of Social Policy Against Family Violence from Colonial Times to the Present*. New York: Oxford University Press.

Pollack, S. & Vaughn, J. (Eds.). 1987. *Politics of the Heart: A Lesbian Parenting Anthology*. Ithaca, NY: Firebrand.

Popenoe, D. 1988. *Disturbing the Nest: Family Change and Decline in Modern Societies*. New York: Alydine de Gruyter.

Price, J. 1988. *Motherhood: What It Does to Your Mind*. London: Pandora Press.

Pruitt, D.G. 1981. *Negotiation Behavior*. New York: Academic Press.

Rosenberg, M. & Kaplan, H.B. (Eds.). 1982. *Social Psychology of the Self-Concept*. Arlington Heights, IL: Harlan Davidson.

Rossi, A.S. & Rossi, P.H. 1990. *Of Human Bonding: Parent-Child Relationships Across the Life-Course*. New York: Alydine de Gruyter.

Rubin, L. 1983. *Intimate Strangers: Men and Women Together*. New York: Harper & Row.

Rubin, L. 1976. *Worlds of Pain: Life in the Working Class Family*. New York: Basic Books.

Russell, G.W. (Ed.). 1988. *Violence in Intimate Relationships*. New York: PMA.

Sampson, R.J. 1988. "Local friendship ties and community attachment in mass society." *American Sociological Review, 53*, 752-766.

Sanders, G.F. & Trystad, D.W. 1989. "Stepgrandparents and grandparents: The view from young adults." *Family Relations, 38*, 71-75.

Saxton, L.S. 1990. *The Individual, Marriage, and the Family*. Belmont, CA: Wadsworth.

Schur, E. 1971. *Labeling Deviant Behavior*. New York: Harper & Row.

Shanas, E. & Streib, G.F. (Eds.). 1965. *Social Structure and the Family: Generational Relations.* Englewood Cliffs, NJ: Prentice-Hall.

Simmel, G. [1896-1917] 1950. *The Sociology of Georg Simmel* (K.H. Wolff, Ed./Trans.). New York: Free Press.

Skolnick, A.S. & Skolnick, J.H. 1989. *Family in Transition: Rethinking Marriage, Sexuality, Child Rearing, and Family Organization.* Glenview, IL: Scott, Foresman.

Slater, P. 1991. *A Dream Deferred–America's Discontent and the Search for a New Democratic Ideal.* Boston: Beacon Press.

Slater, P. 1970. *The Pursuit of Loneliness: American Culture at the Breaking Point.* Boston: Beacon Press.

Small, S.A. & Riley, D. 1990. "Assessment of work spillover into family life." *Journal of Marriage and the Family, 52,* 51-62.

Sprey, J. 1988. "Current theorizing on the family: An appraisal." *Journal of Marriage and the Family, 50,* 875-890.

Stack, C. 1974. *All Our Kin: Strategies for Survival in a Black Community.* New York: Harper & Row.

Staples, R. (Ed.). 1986. *The Black Family: Essays and Studies.* Belmont, CA: Wadsworth.

Steinmetz, S.K. (Ed.). 1988. *Family and Support Systems Across the Life Span.* New York: Plenum.

Steinmetz, S.K. & Straus, M.A. (Eds.). 1974. *Violence in the Family.* New York: Dodd, Mead.

Stoller, E.P. 1990. "Males as helpers: The role of sons, relatives, and friends." *The Gerontologist, 30,* 228-235.

Stoller, E.P. 1983. "Parental caregiving by adult children." *Journal of Marriage and the Family, 45,* 851-858.

Straus, M.A., Gelles, R.J., & Steinmetz, S.K. 1980. *Behind Closed Doors.* Garden City, NY: Doubleday.

Straus, R.A. 1984. "Changing the definition of the situation: Toward a theory of sociological intervention." *Clinical Sociology Review, 2,* 51-63.

Straus, R.A. (Ed.). 1979. Clinical sociology [Special issue]. *American Behavioral Scientist, 22*(4).

Strauss, A. 1978. *Negotiations: Varieties, Contexts, Processes and Social Order.* San Francisco: Jossey-Bass.

Stryker, S. 1968. "Identity salience and role performance." *Journal of Marriage and the Family, 30,* 558-564.

Sussman, M.B. 1953. "The help pattern in the middle-class family." *American Sociological Review, 18,* 22-28.

Sussman, M.B. & Burchinal, L. 1962. "Kin family network: Unheralded structure in current conceptualization of family functioning." *Marriage and Family Living, 24,* 320-332.

Sussman, M.B. & Steinmetz, S.K. (Eds.). 1987. *Handbook of Marriage and the Family.* New York: Plenum Press.

Swan, L.A. 1984. *The Practice of Clinical Sociology and Sociotherapy.* Cambridge, MA: Schenkman.

Teilhard de Chardin, P. 1965. *The Phenomenon of Man.* New York: Harper & Row.

Thomas, D.L. & Cornwall, M. 1990. "Religion and family." *Journal of Marriage and the Family, 52,* 983-992.

Thomas, W.I. 1931. "The relation of research to the social process." In *Essays on Research in the Social Sciences,* edited by L.S. Lyon, I. Lubin, L. Meriam, and P.G. Wright. (pp.175-194). Washington, DC: Brookings Institution.

Thomas, W.I. & Znaniecki, F. 1927. *The Polish Peasant in Europe and America* (Vols. 1 & 2). New York: Knopf.

Thorne, B. & Yalmon, M. (Eds.). 1982. *Rethinking the Family: Some Feminist Questions.* New York: Longman.

Toman, W. 1976. *Family Constellation: Its Effects on Personality and Social Behavior.* New York: Springer.

Turner, R.H. 1970. *Family Interaction.* New York: John Wiley.

von Bertalanffy, L. 1968. *General Systems Theory.* New York: George Braziller.

Wallerstein, J.S. & Kelly, J.B. 1980. *Surviving the Break-Up: How Children and Parents Cope with Divorce.* New York: Basic Books.

Walsh, F. (Ed.). 1982. *Normal Family Processes.* New York: Guilford.

Walters, M., Carter, B., Papp, P., & Silverstein, O. 1988. *The Invisible Web: Gender Patterns in Family Relationships.* New York: Guilford.

Waugh, E.H., Abu-Laban, S.M., & Qureshi, R.G. (Eds.). 1991. *Muslim Families in North America.* Edmonton: University of Alberta Press.

Weitzman, L. 1985. *The Divorce Revolution: The Unexpected Social and Economic Consequences for Women and Children in America.* New York: Free Press.

Wentworth, W. 1980. *Context and Understanding: An Inquiry into Socialization Theory.* New York: Elsevier.

White, B.B. 1989. "Gender differences in marital communication patterns." *Family Process, 28,* 89-106.

Wilson, E.O. 1980. *Sociobiology.* Cambridge, MA: Harvard University Press.

Wirth, L. 1931. "Clinical sociology." *American Journal of Sociology, 37,* 49-66.

York, P., York, D., & Wachtel, T. 1982. *Toughlove.* New York: Doubleday.

Young, M.D. & Wilmott, P. 1973. *The Symmetrical Family: A Study of Work and Leisure in the London Region.* London: Routledge & Kegan Paul.

Zavella, P. 1987. *Women's Work and Chicano Families: Cannery Workers of the Santa Clara Valley.* Ithaca, NY: Cornell University Press.

Zurcher, L. 1983. *Social Roles: Conformity, Conflict and Creativity.* Beverly Hills, CA: Sage.

Index

Adopted child, 76-77
Age roles, 153,154,155
Alternative families, 27-28
Ancestors. *See* Intergenerational
    family systems
Angela (family bonding life history),
    95-96
Art forms in family bonding, 91
Authority. *See* Structure of family
Authors in family history, 53-55
Autonomy. *See* Independence

Behavior and behavior changes
    abandoning negative
    as consequence of identity, 45-47
    crisis and, 67,73
    family reaction to, 47-48
    in life-giving families, 39
    in smother-love families, 38
    values and, 47
Beliefs. *See* Values
Biological child, 76
Birth, role of family in, 100-102
Birth order, 76,77
Bowen, Murray, 150

Caring for families, 28-29
Caring in families
    consequences of, 33-34,39
    contrasts in, 34-35
    emotional system, 36-37
    empty families, 38
    fulfillment and, 36
    life-giving families, 38-39
    smother-love families, 37-38

Celebrations in family bonding, 94
Changes in behavior
    crisis and, 67,73
    family reaction to, 13
    family support in, 26
    letting go of negative aspects,
        129-130
Child care, 4-5
Children
    adopted and biological, 75-76
    birth, 100-102
    death of, 71-72
    parents and, 80-81
    pictures in family bonding, 91
    poetry in family bonding, 90
    in smother-love families, 37-38
Choices
    in creating new family, 117
    finding joy in families, 119-120
    about values and behaviors, 13-14
Clinical interventions in study, 151
Closed families
    family events in, 99-100
    traditional families as, 153
Communication
    about wills, 112-113
    in empty families, 38
    in family bonding, 89-94
    family secrets, 52-53
    as giving, 139
    in life-giving families, 39
    in smother-love families, 38
Conditioning, choices about, 13
Conflicts
    constructive, 137-138
    in empty families, 38
    questions about, 18-19

making a will in, 114
practical steps, 58-60

Gays. *See* Homosexuals
Gender roles
    birth, 101
    in death, 103
    families and, 3
    flexibility, 3-5
    new families, 155
    in new families, 130-131,145-146
    in nuclear families, 154
    in relationships between men and
        women, 18,136-137
    in traditional families, 153
Geoffrey (family life cycle transition
    life history), 105-106
Geographical distance. *See* Physical
    distance
Giving to our families, 20,139
Goals
    autonomy and, 60-61
    family conflicts and, 137
    family history and, 60
    in new families, 145
    questions about, 16-17
    in self-development, 134-135
    in smother-love families, 38
    transcendent, 117-118
Government policy, 9
Graham (family history compilation
    life history), 54

Harry (death of a parent life history),
    70-71
Hazel (family history compilation
    life history), 55
Helen (positive family patterns life
    history), 30
Helping behavior in families, 15
Herbert and Lilian (death of a child
    life history), 71-72
Heterosexuals, 78-79

Hierarchical family structure
    future of, 140
    male-dominated versus egalitarian,
        10-11
    in nuclear families, 154
    questions about, 16
Homosexuals
    family reaction to, 82-85
    family status and emotional
        system, 79

Ideal type profiles
    defined, 152
    new families, 154-155
    nuclear families, 154
    traditional families, 153
Identity
    behavioral consequences, 41,
        45-47
    determining facts about ourselves,
        42-43
    family as source of, 3, 43-44
    family history in determining,
        55-56,57
    family relationships in,
        44-45,125-126
    mythology of others' impressions,
        41-42
    tasks for defining, 47-48
Identity empowerment theory, 150
Income, 33
Independence, *See also* Fulfillment
    crises and, 69
    dependencies and, 122-123
    emotional system and, 36-37,39
    families in giving, 26-27
    family interaction in, 5-6,122-123,
        129
    future-oriented actions, 60-63
    goals in, 60-61
    in life-giving families, 38-39
    making a will and, 113-114
    as meeting family needs, 33
    selecting from family values, 128